"One of the most moving scenes in all four Gospels is in the home of someone in Emmaus. The two walkers implored Jesus, whom they had not yet recognized, to stay with them. So Jesus did. At the table that night Jesus, with the bread in his hands, thanked God and then broke it. In the act of breaking bread, in the home, the eyes of the two disciples were opened and they perceived the truth of who Jesus was—their crucified and resurrected Lord. In a home, over bread—nothing could be more common and more revelatory. Homes matter, for in them God breaks through. *The Hunger for Home*, scene after scene, reveals how home slakes our thirsts and satisfies our deepest longings."

—**Scot McKnight**, *Professor of New Testament, Northern Seminary*

"This book will help you to find deeper meaning in something you do every single day. Croasmun and Volf explore how the seemingly ordinary act of eating is an extraordinary occasion for mutual care and encounter with the living God. By bringing the meals of Luke's Gospel to life, Croasmun and Volf explain why being at home with one another and with God is possible every day and closer at hand than we thought."

—**Angela W. Gorrell**, *Assistant Professor of Practical Theology, Truett Theological Seminary, Baylor University*

"By walking us through the Gospel of Luke, Croasmun and Volf help us see why the meals we eat, and who we share them with, should be a foretaste of our eternal home. The result is a very practical, and very moving, book—indeed, I would say that reading the book is itself a spiritual exercise. I warmly recommend it, therefore, to pastors, church groups, theologians, or anyone else who is trying to live a faithful life."

—**Kevin W. Hector**, *Professor of Theology and of the Philosophy of Religions, University of Chicago*

"If you're looking for a retreat or small group book on eating practices and Christian discipleship, this is it. Plenty has been written on ancient meal practices in the Gospels, not all of it accessible to broad audiences. *The Hunger for Home* offers a provocative, historically informed meditation on meals in Luke that can be enjoyed by novice and expert alike—alone or with others, in a day, a week, or a month."

—**Sonja Anderson**, *Assistant Professor of Religion, Carleton College*

"I have been reading and studying the Scriptures for almost fifty years on a near-daily basis. *The Hunger for Home* offered the rare experience in which, on numerous occasions, I thought 'I've never considered that intertextual connection before' and 'I've never had this biblical text explained in such a fresh way!' I highly recommend *The Hunger for Home* for small groups and for personal devotional study. It is a spiritual feast."

—**Rich Nathan**, *Founding Pastor, Vineyard Columbus*

The
HUNGER
for
HOME

Food and Meals in the
Gospel of Luke

Matthew Croasmun & **Miroslav Volf**

Baylor University Press

Unless otherwise stated, Scripture quotations are from the New Revised Standard Version Bible, copyright 1989, Division of Christian Education of the National Council of the Churches of Christ in the United States of America. Used by permission. All rights reserved.

Cover and book design by Kasey McBeath
Cover art © Shutterstock/Potapov Alexander

Library of Congress Cataloging-in-Publication Data

Names: Croasmun, Matthew, 1979- author. | Volf, Miroslav, author.

Title: The hunger for home : food and meals in the Gospel of Luke / Matthew Croasmun, Miroslav Volf.

Description: Waco : Baylor University Press, 2022. | Includes bibliographical references. | Summary: "Through a set of passages focused on the theme of food in the Gospel of Luke, Croasmun and Volf offer readers a vision of a meal as the quintessential enactment of home: a site of nourishing mutual encounter between people, places, and God that makes present the eschatological home that it represents"-- Provided by publisher.

Identifiers: LCCN 2022008857 (print) | LCCN 2022008858 (ebook) | ISBN 9781481317665 (cloth) | ISBN 9781481317696 (pdf) | ISBN 9781481317689 (epub)

Subjects: LCSH: Bible. Luke--Criticism, interpretation, etc. | Dinners and dining in the Bible. | Home--Religious aspects--Christianity. | Kingdom of God.

Classification: LCC BS2595.6.D56 C76 2022 (print) | LCC BS2595.6.D56 (ebook) | DDC 226.4/06--dc23/eng/20220502

LC record available at https://lccn.loc.gov/2022008857

LC ebook record available at https://lccn.loc.gov/2022008858

Contents

Introduction   1

  1 Not by Bread Alone, Not without Bread   11

  2 Feasting in the Fields   27

  3 Sinners at the Table   43

  4 Rich and Poor at the Table   61

  5 Dining at Home   75

  6 Made Known in the Breaking of the Bread   91

Acknowledgments   105
Works Cited   107

Introduction

The hunger for home sums up our hearts' deepest longings. Temporally, this hunger seems to pull us in both directions at once. Home is the object of nostalgia (*The Wizard of Oz*'s "there's no place like home") and yet also the focus of our most imaginative hopes (*West Side Story*'s "Somewhere"). Whether we're trying to find our way back home or convinced that we're looking for a home we've never known, the longing for home captures this orientation of the human heart: "back" to a past yet to be realized, "forward" to become what we've always been intended to be from the beginning. The hunger for home is return and advent intertwined. It is memory and imagination. Restoration and transformation. Creation and consummation.

As such, it captures both the "backward" and "forward" of the Christian tradition. Home is what grounds the entire trajectory from Eden to the New Jerusalem: the world at home in having become the home of God. (We elaborate on this trajectory in *For the Life of the World: Theology That Makes a Difference*, 68–71.)

Yet, as the saying goes, the path to the human heart is through the stomach. There are perhaps few stronger memories of home, few things that can bring us more intimately back to our homes of origin, than the smell of a favorite food. Even one whiff can bring to mind a whole set of relations that extend beyond any food or any one meal but are at the same time evoked by and implicated in any meal that took place there.

Luke's prodigal's return is driven by a literal *hunger for home*. His desire to return begins with a hunger so profound that he longed even to eat the food he was feeding the pigs. The memory of the way his father provided ample food even for the workers triggers a powerful desire to return to the father's home. Sure enough, when the prodigal returns home, he is greeted with a meal. As much as it is effected in his father's embrace and gift of a ring, the prodigal's return is realized also in his nostrils, in the familiar smell of home cooking. The return home is sealed in a *meal*: in the tastes, smells, physical touch, companionship, and relations with all those who belong to this home, in sharing the fruits of *this* particular land, cared for and cultivated by *these* people, at the invitation of the father whose embrace constitutes this extravagant home.

The claim here, if we have ears to hear, is this: the home of God, too, is enacted in a meal. There are tastes and smells of the home of God. As Luke presents him, Jesus is the herald of the home of God, made known in his invitation to the table.

————

In Luke chapter 4, having received the Holy Spirit, Jesus returns home to Nazareth. Or so it was thought. Twice in the passage, Jesus names Nazareth as his "hometown." The Greek word is *patris*, and one can recognize the connection to *fatherhood* that this appellation entails. Nazareth is the land of Joseph, the man *thought to be* Jesus' father (3:23). Nazareth is, like Joseph, irreducible to understanding Jesus. And yet Jesus' home is in no way reducible to Nazareth.

The teaching Jesus gives in Nazareth and the conflict that follows are about a more powerful vision of home. In the hometown synagogue, called on to read the *haftarah* (the "lectionary" readings from the prophets), Jesus declares forthrightly the purpose for which the Spirit has come upon him by reciting the words of Isaiah:

The Spirit of the Lord is upon me,
> because he has anointed me
> to bring good news to the poor.
He has sent me to proclaim release to the captives
> and recovery of sight to the blind,
> to let the oppressed go free,
to proclaim the year of the Lord's favor. (4:18-19)

The recitation is largely from Isaiah 61:1-2, though "to let the oppressed go free" is borrowed from Isaiah 58:6. Each of these intertexts contributes more than just the words recited. Together, they clearly invoke themes of Jubilee, repeating the Greek word for "release." (The Greek translation of Leviticus 25:10 calls the Jubilee year a "year of release.") "Release" is a key theme in Luke. Jesus' healing ministry is depicted as *release from the binding power of Satan* (13:10-17). Forgiveness is primarily understood as *release from sin*, which is itself figured as a *release from debts* (11:4). And Luke's interest in debt forgiveness extends beyond this metaphorical use to those straining under the thumb of creditors (1:46-55). The Jubilee that Jesus has come to declare is marked by release from sin, illness, and debt.

This Jubilee release is not a matter of declaration only. There is a Jubilee way of life, a way of *enacting* the release declared. Isaiah 58:6-7 describes it especially vividly:

> Is not this the fast that I choose:
>> to loose the bonds of injustice,
>> to undo the thongs of the yoke,
>> to let the oppressed go free,
>> and to break every yoke?
> Is it not to share your bread with the hungry,
>> and bring the homeless poor into your house;
>> when you see the naked, to cover them,
>> and not to hide yourself from your own kin?

Feeding the hungry and welcoming the poor, too, mark the ministry of Jesus and that of his followers in Luke. Jesus both declares and enacts the Jubilee.

This Jubilee release, declared and enacted, makes possible a new sort of home. There is a reign of justice (Isa 61:8). People live in secure dwellings (Isa 58:12, 61:4). There are proper relations among people and to the land (Isa 61:11). And there is joy and gladness where there was mourning (Isa 61:3, 7). In this home, life flourishes in the presence of the living God, whose Spirit occasions this transformation (Isa 61:1). Relatedness to God stands at the center of flourishing relationships in this home such that those who belong to this home are known as "priests of the LORD" (Isa 61:6).

When Jesus says of Isaiah 61, "Today this scripture has been fulfilled in your hearing" (Luke 4:21), his meaning is plain. He has come to declare the eschatological (that is, the final, end-times) Jubilee and set the land and the people free. He has come to call God's people home. He has come to cast vision for a future that realizes the hopes of a past they may have forgotten. He has come to invite them to remember a future long ago promised. He has come to enact the longed-for eschatological home in their midst.

The focal expression of that eschatological home is a *feast*. This much would have been clear to Jesus' audience. The expectation of a Messianic banquet is expressed in prophetic texts like Isaiah 25:6-8:

> On this mountain the LORD of hosts will make for all peoples
>   a feast of rich food, a feast of well-aged wines,
>   of rich food filled with marrow, of well-aged wines
>   strained clear.
> And he will destroy on this mountain
>   the shroud that is cast over all peoples,

> the sheet that is spread over all nations;
>> he will swallow up death forever.
> Then the Lord GOD will wipe away the tears from all faces,
>> and the disgrace of his people he will take away from all
>>> the earth,
>> for the LORD has spoken.

Isaiah 61 itself, from which Jesus reads in the Nazareth synagogue, invokes this expectation by using the image of a wedding banquet (Isa 61:10). As Jesus inaugurates the kingdom of God, he issues an invitation to the banquet of the kingdom.

At first, the reception is positive (Luke 4:22a). The trouble is that the scope and nature of this home challenges the existing structures of home in Nazareth. The centrality of Jesus as herald of this new home troubles his identity in his hometown. "Is not this Joseph's son?" asks the crowd (4:22b). As Luke says and we noted above, so it was thought (3:23). Inasmuch as the Nazareth home is embedded within the larger home of the people of God in Judea—and just this embeddedness is enacted in the synagogue service in which Jesus is speaking—Nazareth indeed is his *patris*; Jesus is herald of the dawn of the home that the God of Israel has promised. And yet, for Jesus, as for Isaiah, the home that the God of Israel has promised has implications beyond the boundaries of Israel. The embrace of this home includes the widow at Zarephath and Naaman the Syrian (4:26-27). Nazareth of Judea is an essential aspect of Jesus' home, essential even to that home that he has come to inaugurate. But his home is not reducible to Nazareth. Allegiance to this expansive home leaves Jesus without honor in his hometown. More importantly, it leaves many in his hometown in danger of missing out on his invitation to the home of God coming to be in their midst.

The possibility of some finding themselves on the outside of the broad invitation to the eschatological table finds explicit expression in Luke 13:28-30. Here again, Jesus leans into the irony that the breadth of God's invitation may nevertheless coincide with some presumed "insiders" placing themselves outside the meal. Abraham, Isaac, and Jacob will be in the kingdom of God, while some of Jesus' hearers are outside. "Then people will come from east and west, from north and south, and will eat in the kingdom of God" (13:29). The home enacted at the table has a scandalously broad embrace. Those in Jesus' hometown will not be the last to ironically exclude themselves because they stumble over the breadth of Jesus' invitation.

Nevertheless, Jesus has announced his mission: to inaugurate this home, to invite people to the kingdom and its feast. To do so, he must declare and enact the Jubilee and call others to do the same. Those of us who would follow him are called to give food to the hungry and to welcome the homeless poor into our houses as partial enactments of the eschatological home coming to be in our midst.

———

Because of the connection between Jesus' mission and the image of the feast, Jesus is throughout Luke the one "made known in the breaking of the bread" (24:35). The nature of the home he is declaring—the Jubilee home to which we are invited—is revealed in a seemingly unceasing series of meals and teachings about food throughout the Gospel. A meal, it turns out, is the quintessential enactment of home, a site of nourishing mutual encounter between people, places, and God that, in ideal circumstances, makes present, in a broken but nevertheless real way, the eschatological home that it represents. At their best—as they are when Jesus is the one inviting people to the table—meals are anticipations of the kingdom. And even when they are less than they ought to be, meals nevertheless reveal the ways in which we have been un-homed. In such experiences of being un-homed, meals can become moments in which we can see the ways God is welcoming us to be at home with one another and with God and the ways God is remaking the larger contexts in which our homes exist.

All this may seem a bit far-fetched at the moment. The rest of the book, we hope, will make it more believable. For now, we simply want to be prepared to notice the way that, as Jesus is made known in the breaking of the bread, he is at the same time revealing the nature of the home to which we are invited. Sometimes this will feel like remembering a home we once knew, even if or precisely because we can't quite place our "memory" of being at home. Sometimes it will feel like the exhilarating imagination of an entirely new world. Sometimes it will feel like both at once. This is what it is to be beckoned home as we are invited to the table.

————

A couple of notes on how to read this book:

1. Read from Luke first. We will list the key passages from Luke that we'll be discussing. You'll get the most out of this book if you read those passages from Luke before

reading our chapter. You might even begin by reading the whole of Luke's Gospel at a single sitting. Close reading is tremendously valuable, but sometimes we can miss the forest for the trees.

2. Read together with a group. As we will see in what follows, feasts are meant to be shared. Scripture, too, is a feast. Consider reading Luke and this book together with a group. There are discussion questions at the end of each chapter to spur conversation and a prayer you might pray together at the end of your group time.

1

Not by Bread Alone,
Not without Bread

Luke 4:1-13, 5:1-11, 9:1-22

One of Matt's friends has a slogan for his approach to a strategy game they both enjoy: "First, I gotta get my bread right." By "bread," he means *money*. In the game, it turns out to be advantageous to first focus on getting your money situation sorted before applying your attention elsewhere. Doubtless, the game is modeling something many of us believe true about the real world. As we will see, Luke insists that Jesus sees things differently.

In a deeper sense, this slogan is an important one for our reading of Luke. If we're going to understand what Luke is trying to tell us about God, about Jesus, about the world and this home into which the many meals of Luke's Gospel invite us, first, we need to get "bread" right. As Luke narrates the adult ministry of Jesus, one of the very first scenes has everything to do with bread: what it is, what it is not, what it is and is not *for*.

———

Full of the Holy Spirit, Jesus is led by the Spirit into the wilderness, where for forty days he is tempted by the devil. During these forty days, Luke doesn't say that Jesus is fasting, simply that he does not eat. Either way, he is famished. It is at this point that the devil approaches and issues what is traditionally considered the "first temptation." As Luke tells it, Jesus has already been undergoing temptation for forty days. This is the first temptation Luke narrates, but, in it, the devil attempts to seize upon an opening made available in Jesus' irrepressible craving for food and his physical and (the devil hopes) spiritual exhaustion.

"If you are the Son of God, command this stone to become a loaf of bread" (4:3). The devil sets the stakes high, and his strategy exploits Jesus' very identity, the foundation God had laid in Jesus' baptism (3:22). Before Jesus begins his work (cf. 3:23), God affirms Jesus' sonship and belovedness. The devil draws this unconditional identity into doubt: *prove* your sonship by a deed of power to relieve your current deepest affliction. Demonstrate your sonship by miraculously producing the means of life and satisfying your hunger.

This question of identity isn't just a mind game the devil is trying to play in Jesus' head. It swirls around Jesus throughout his life. Herod wants to know who he is. The crowds are trying to figure it out. Jesus polls his disciples. And, again and again in Luke, Jesus is made known through bread—present, absent, what have you. This first encounter is no exception.

Jesus responds, as he does to each temptation, with the words of Hebrew scripture: "One does not live by bread alone" (4:4). The reference is to Deuteronomy 8:3: "He humbled you by letting you hunger, then by feeding you with manna, with which neither you nor your ancestors were acquainted, in order to make you understand that one does not live by bread alone, but by every word that comes from the mouth of the LORD." God can satisfy hunger by providing bread even in the wilderness. But there's a lesson to be learned. The purpose of the feeding was so that the people might understand that the human does not live by bread alone. It is this lesson that Jesus cites and, with it, invokes the entire scenario.

"One does not live by bread alone." The scriptural citation drops off before it's complete. The elision invites a response. "One does not live by bread alone," says Jesus. "But by every word which comes from the mouth of the Lord," the devil is forced to answer. Far from concealing what is omitted, to the contrary, for the devil and for Luke's reader, the "call and response" places *emphasis* on what is not there. In this case, our imaginations are to be filled with memories of provision wrought by the creative word of God. The word that brought manna in the desert. The word that said in Genesis "let there be," and there was.

Human life is not by bread alone. We live not by bread alone but also by the life-giving and life-sustaining words of the God who spoke the world into being. God's life-giving relation to us is not an add-on to a life already amply sustained by plentiful food. Prone as we are to gloss "relating to God" as some sort of "self-actualization," we can be tempted to think about relating to God as a "nice to have" after the basics of life are dealt with. Perhaps we can blame Maslow and his ubiquitous hierarchy of needs. But the "higher" aspects of our lives—questions of meaning, purpose, and worth—do not wait for us first to sort out the material foundations of our lives; if they did, they would always remain waiting, for we are "never enough" people living in a "never enough" system. As Jesus implies, our relatedness to God—God's life-giving relation to us—does not start only after we "graduate" from the basics of life to begin asking these profoundly human questions about meaning and purpose. We are fed by God from the very start.

We misunderstand human life if we reduce it to just bread. But we also misunderstand *bread* if we reduce it to just bread. Bread, whether dramatically as manna from heaven or more prosaically as the fruit of God's good creation cultivated and rendered delectable by the work of human hands, proceeds from the mouth of the Lord. True, according to Genesis 2:5, it takes two, God (who gives rain) and humans (who till the ground), for grain to grow and bread to be made. But humans and their work come from God's word and not just the rain. God speaks and it all comes to be: grain and laboring humans. A loaf of bread is the most ordinary and most miraculous of things. Bread is an artifact of particular creative potencies latent in the goodness of the interrelatedness of God's creation. It results from and sustains a set of relations between God, peoples, and the whole of creation. All three are made at home with one another in bread that is not just bread. As mere bread, bread is no more than fuel to sustain the human body. When we make bread preferable to the God who provides it, when we make it into mere fuel to sustain our bodies, it alienates us from this home. In rebuffing Satan's temptation, Jesus refuses this alienation.

Neither Jesus nor Deuteronomy says that the human lives without bread. Without food, we die. Jesus' forty days without food aren't a challenge to that basic fact but rather serve to heighten his and our awareness of it in his *hunger*. The NRSV says he is *famished*. We need food to live. We need bread to survive. In insisting that bread is more than mere bread, Jesus is helping us interpret our hunger, helping us make sense of our fundamental insufficiency in ourselves that our need to eat affirms every day. Our need for food teaches us of our need for God, God's creation, and God's people. It is no mere *analogy* to say that as the deer pants for water, so our soul longs for God (Ps 42:1). The very bodily longing of hunger *is*, if we can see it rightly, a longing for God and God's gifts. We can be fully satisfied only when every bite of bread we take feeds both our hunger for food and our hunger for God.

———

We should admit that, to many of us, mere bread has its appeals. Our daily striving after the means of life—money, health, education, and all the rest—often proceeds without thought or reference to the divine source of these things or God's good purposes in them. We postpone such weighty questions until after we've got these "basics" secured. Doing so strikes us as the "responsible," even "dutiful," thing to do. There's something honorable about putting in a hard day's work and walking away with sustenance for ourselves and for our families. Often, it's hardly glamorous, but someone needs to, as we say, put food on the table. Surely we needn't apologize if theology has to take a back seat while we attend to the means of life. After all, even in paradise, Adam and Eve did the ordinary work of "tilling and keeping" (Gen 2:15).

Simon's work was not glamorous. One of his first encounters with Jesus came at perhaps the least glamorous moment of his daily routine: washing his nets after a fruitless night of fishing. Lest we romanticize the lives of these fishermen as some sort of first-century middle-class entrepreneurs, we should note that fishing was fully integrated into the patronage system, mediated by tax collectors, that dominated the entire Greco-Roman world. The lake was owned by royal elites who sold fishing rights, through various tax-collecting middlemen, to syndicates who contracted with families who would fish. Fishing rights were expensive, which left fishermen like Simon indebted, needing to meet quotas to pay what they owed. The way Luke tells it, Simon is on the shore attending to this chore when Jesus climbs into his boat without him. Jesus is already in the boat when he asks Simon to join him and to "put out a little way from the shore" (5:3). Jesus' chutzpah becomes shameless audacity when, after he finishes teaching, he tells Simon, who just spent all night fishing and has come up empty, to put down his nets for a catch. The boat—and those of Simon's companions—almost sinks under the weight of the catch. In an instant, Luke begins calling Simon by the name Jesus would give him. When he saw the catch, "Simon Peter . . . fell down at Jesus' knees, saying, 'Go away from me, Lord, for I am a sinful man!'" (5:8).

What has happened to Simon in this moment? His world is coming apart like one domino falling after another. First, his entire relationship to the means of life—to the daily work of his livelihood—is radically relativized by the fish swamping his boat. How many nights has he spent laboring just to try to haul in enough of a catch to make ends meet? And, in an instant, his *labor* is pushed to the margins, at least for the time being. Many nights of work could not have produced this yield (even if most of the proceeds would go to the tax man). One does not live by labor alone as one does not live by bread alone.

That means, further, that Simon's entire relationship to the results of his work is primarily a matter of a *gift received* rather than *wages earned*. Even when we labor for bread—or, in this case, fish—it still comes from the mouth of the Lord. Another seductive aspect of mere bread is undone in Simon's encounter with Jesus. Mere bread can become for us bread we *own*, to which we are entitled—bread we *deserve*. For Simon, fish were interwoven into a vast network of ownership, indebtedness, wages, and, hopefully, at the end of the day, some just deserts for all his labor. Bread as a mere object of exchange—owed, earned, bought and paid for—alienates us from the home into which *real* bread invites us, bread perceived as more than mere bread. But here Simon is, overwhelmed by an abundance he would previously have imagined to be the fruit of the sweat of his brow, the debt owed the taxman—except here it is, in spite of, rather than because of, all the sweat of the night before. He didn't *earn* these fish. But, then, maybe no one has ever strictly *earned* a fish, *owed* a fish, or *been owed* a fish. Maybe all of it has always been gift. And from there, the dominoes just continue to fall. If fish are gifts—not debts owed or reprieve from indebtedness earned—then what of the rest of his life? Simon's life comes apart in a cascading realization of undeserved blessedness.

But, as in Deuteronomy, the most revelatory aspect of this encounter is not the abundance of fish but rather their *source:* the *word* of this miraculous teacher. As the Israelites gain insight into the nature of the Lord God in the abundant provision of manna in the desert, so Simon gains insight into the nature of Jesus as Lord in the miraculous catch of fish. "We have worked all night long but have caught nothing," Simon laments. It is when he concedes, "Yet if you say so," that everything changes. The lesson is plain: one does not live by bread (or fish) alone, but by every word that proceeds from the mouth of *this* Lord.

The words that provide abundant fish ("Put out into the deep water and let down your nets for a catch," in v. 4) are swiftly followed by words that lead Simon beyond fish: "Do not be afraid; from now on you will be catching people" (5:10). This is an invitation to a life that aims far beyond mere provision of the means of life, toward calling people together into life-giving relationship with God and with one another. And, as we will soon see, it involves no small amount of fish. Human life is not by fish alone and not by work alone, but, especially in the material context of these small fishing villages and the wilderness that surrounds them, human life is also surely not without fish and without work. And fish, too, as it turns out, are more than mere fish, and work more than mere work. As food, fish, too, are gifts and, as such, sites of relationship. And the same is true of work. In this sense, Jesus' extension of Simon's vocation from fishing-for-fish to fishing-for-people isn't just a clever turn of phrase. The invitation to community building points to a deeper sense of Simon's original vocation: tending to the networks of relationship that were always implied in the pursuit of fish that are not merely fish.

These two early passages in the adult ministry of Jesus form something of a pair. In the temptation Jesus says to us: Don't get lost in mere bread; bread is more than mere bread. It is an invitation to life with God in God's good creation. I prefer hunger to bread that is mere bread. And, in the calling of Simon, Jesus again says: Don't get lost in mere work; see, I can provide more of its fruits than you could ever need. Don't believe you can secure it; receive your work and your provision as a gift. Learn the lesson of the manna; understand that you live not by bread alone and not by work alone but by every word that proceeds from my mouth. That has always been true of your "quotidian" work; what if we named the gratuity of creation and deliberately built a way of life upon it?

———

The devil's bread-temptation was phrased as a challenge to Jesus' identity. In Luke 9, the questions are still swirling around. Miracles are reported to Herod, along with theories about Jesus' identity: perhaps John had been raised, or Elijah or another of the ancient prophets had appeared (9:7-9). That this is the "word on the street" is confirmed just ten verses later, as Luke reports Jesus' disciples relaying the same set of guesses about Jesus' identity among the crowds that follow him (9:19). In v. 20, Simon Peter proffers an insight: Jesus is the "Messiah of God." This is not a secret to the reader of Luke. Jesus has been identified as such from birth (2:11, 26). But since then, in the Gospel itself, this has been a dangerous secret. Aside from in an exegetical puzzle proposed by Jesus about "the Messiah" in the abstract in 20:41, the title won't appear again until the trials and crucifixion. After the resurrection, as we will see, the title "Messiah" is at the center of the puzzle that needs to be pieced together.

What has happened between these two rehearsals of the popular confusion about the identity of Jesus? A meal. Jesus has been made known in the breaking of the bread.

The setup seems almost deliberate. Jesus had sent out his disciples to proclaim and to demonstrate the kingdom of God, deputizing them to share in his work. On this trip, he instructed them to take nothing for their journey, "no staff, nor bag, nor bread, nor money—not even an extra tunic" (9:3). They are to depend on the hospitality of those among whom they minister. So it is no surprise that, upon returning from their journey, faced with feeding an enormous crowd who has followed Jesus to a deserted place, the disciples are nearly empty-handed.

The disciples devise a simple strategy: "Send the crowd away, so that they may go into the surrounding villages and countryside, to lodge and get provisions" (9:12). But Jesus continues his training of the disciples: "You give them something to eat" (9:13). Peter had his miraculous catch of fish. Now it's time for him and the rest of the disciples to be on the giving end of things, proclaiming and demonstrating the generosity of God in the abundance of God's good gifts.

The disciples have just five loaves of bread and two fish, a comically small amount to feed this crowd of more than 5,000. But Jesus asks the disciples to have the crowd sit down in groups of fifty, blesses and breaks the bread and fish, and gives them to the disciples to give to the crowd. Everyone eats their fill, and the disciples collect basketfuls of leftovers.

The scene auditions each of the proposed identities of Jesus in the surrounding passages. Like John the Baptist, Jesus is gathering crowds in the desert who are eager to hear his preaching. But the miraculous provision of food suggests that, as John himself suggested when the crowd was wondering whether John might be the Messiah, Jesus is someone much more powerful (cf. 3:15-16).

The miraculous provision of bread might remind us of Elijah's provision of bread for the widow at Zarephath (1 Kgs 17:8-16). Or perhaps the closest parallel is Elisha's miracle recorded in 2 Kings 4:42-44:

> A man came from Baal-shalishah, bringing food from the first fruits to the man of God: twenty loaves of barley and fresh ears of grain in his sack. Elisha said, "Give it to

> the people and let them eat." But his servant said, "How can I set this before a hundred people?" So he repeated, "Give it to the people and let them eat, for thus says the LORD, 'They shall eat and have some left.'" He set it before them, they ate, and had some left, according to the word of the LORD.

No wonder the people say perhaps Jesus is Elijah or another of the ancient prophets returned.

Even more plainly, the scene is also a recapitulation of the original provision of manna, which, since Luke 4, we, the readers, have been prepared to recognize. The deserted place recalls the wandering in the desert. The groups of fifty may recall the organization of the people of Israel during the Exodus (Exod 18:21, 25). As commentator François Bovon notes: "The setting of the episode in the wilderness reminds Israel of their origins as a lost and wandering people, and of God's protection. God took their hunger seriously, and responded to the need at that time, but not in a natural way: he gave his people 'earthly' goods through a 'heavenly' gift: manna and quail" (359). God provides bread that is not mere bread and fish that are not mere fish. Bovon goes on to connect the fish to these miraculous quails, which, having risen up from the direction of the sea, are like "flying fish." Bovon concludes: "Jesus is thus not only a prophet like Elisha or Elijah, but also the last prophet like Moses" (359).

But Exodus goes to great lengths to distinguish between Yahweh, the source of heavenly food, and Moses and Aaron, who are mere intermediaries of this provision (Exod 16:6-8). (Similarly, in 2 Kings 4 above, Elisha is careful to offer a prophetic saying of the Lord that distinguishes his facilitation of the miracle from the Lord's miraculous word itself.) Taking a more careful look at the provision of manna and the feeding of the 5,000, it is not Jesus who plays the role of Moses and Aaron but rather the disciples. While Jesus looks to heaven and blesses the bread and the fish, like the miraculous catch of fish, the entire scene proceeds according to *his* word. Jesus is not Moses; he is the Lord from whom come the words—and the bread—by which one lives.

Is Jesus John the Baptist? No, he is more than just a teacher in the desert to whom crowds flock. Is he Elijah or another of the ancient prophets? Not only; he is more than just a medium of God's miraculous provision. If the identifications of Jesus proposed to Herod made any sense earlier in chapter 9, Luke knocks them all down one by one, even as he uses them to weave a tapestry of identity markers that build upon and point beyond themselves.

By the time the disciples rehearse the same set of popular hypotheses about Jesus' identity in 9:19, their insufficiency is plain. We the readers are prepared to recognize Peter's insight: Jesus is the Messiah of God—a Messiah beyond anyone's expectation.

———

In two passages in the wilderness (the temptation and the feeding), Luke invokes the miraculous provision of manna in the desert as a key for understanding the identity of Jesus. From the very beginning in temptation, Luke proposes the interpretive key to make sense of this intertext: the human does not live by bread alone, but by every word that proceeds from the mouth of the Lord (Deut 8:3). The miraculous catch of fish and, even more so, the feeding of the 5,000 make clear: Jesus is this Lord from whom come life-sustaining words. There is no competition between the Lord and the food we need to live.

Jesus summarizes this relationship between created goods and God through whom they come as he begins to teach his disciples to pray in Luke 11:2-3: "Father, hallowed be your name. Your kingdom come. Give us each day our daily bread." God is set apart, hallowed, holy. And yet God has bound Godself to all that is not God in a dynamic relationship of abundant life: the kingdom of God. It is in this network of relations in the Father's home that we find our daily bread. We need it. We need it daily. The regularity and existential stakes of this need can tempt us to pursue bread outside of the kingdom (12:30). This is to settle for mere bread. True bread by which we live comes from the Father through the kingdom—this world-becoming-true-home inaugurated in the presence of the living Christ.

"Strive for the kingdom," Jesus says, "and these things will be given to you as well" (12:31). He does not mean food, clothing, and drink will be tossed in along with the kingdom, like freebies at the supermarket. Daily bread cannot be added alongside the kingdom. The true sustenance we need—the material world rendered more than mere materiality—is precisely these material goods in dynamic relation to God and to one another: that is, the kingdom. If we dare to seek this true daily bread, we can be confident as we do, as Jesus assures us: "Do not be afraid, little flock, for it is your Father's good pleasure to give you the kingdom" (12:32).

DISCUSSION QUESTIONS

1. Where in our world do you recognize a preference for "mere bread"? In what ways are you tempted to pursue "mere bread"?

2. Our economic lives seem to be structured around what is systematically treated as mere work for mere bread. Can you think of ways to infuse your work with a sense of it being a gift and collaboration with God in God's project?

3. In what ways has God invited you to participate in Jesus' work of announcing the abundance of God's good gifts to the world?

PRAYER

Lord by whose very words we live, let us hunger for bread that is more than just bread. Let us recognize You as the source of every good gift. Let us be united with You in every work we do and hunger we seek to satisfy. Let us dare to share the good news of Your abundant gifts with the world You so love. Amen.

2

Feasting in the Fields

Luke 5:33-35, 6:1-5, 20:41-44

"In Luke's Gospel, Jesus is either going to a meal, at a meal, or coming from a meal." Robert Karris' comment in his book *Eating Your Way through Luke's Gospel* is an exaggeration but nevertheless offers no small insight into Jesus and his ministry (14). Karris isn't the only one to take notice. The Pharisees and their scribes also have an observation: John the Baptist's disciples, like the Pharisees, "fast and pray, but your disciples eat and drink" (5:33). The comparison of these two pairs, "fast and pray" versus "eat and drink," is not meant to be flattering to Jesus and his disciples. Jesus has an explanation, but for it to make sense, we probably need to recall Jesus' personal mission statement in Luke 4.

There, as we noted in the introduction, Jesus describes his mission in terms of declaring and enacting the year of Jubilee. He does so through a recitation from Isaiah that weaves a fragment from Isaiah 58 into two verses from Isaiah 61. In so doing, Jesus calls to mind for his hearers a whole constellation of biblical images of release: a release of debts, of sins, a liberation from the powers of sickness and the devil—a liberation of the land.

This has everything to do with why his disciples do not fast. "You cannot make wedding guests fast while the bridegroom is with them, can you?" (5:34) Jesus calls to mind another eschatological image present in Isaiah 61:10: the wedding feast. It adds to the growing sense of the character of Jesus' Jubilee mission. The party has begun. The feast is here. Who would declare a *fast*? It would be out of sync with the moment. You have to know what time it is. And you have to know what it means for where you are, for the geographical expansiveness of Jesus' mission cannot be construed apart from its particular orientation and bond to the people of Judea. Now is the inauguration of Jubilee. The land is being set free. The disciples are to declare the good news to the poor, set the oppressed free, release the captives, bring sight to the blind, and declare the year of the Lord's favor. If and as they do so, every meal they eat points toward a feast like no other: a feast that makes present the coming reality of the world set free to find its home in becoming the home of God.

But this feast is not yet here. And, as Jesus indicates, in not too long, Jesus, the bridegroom, will no longer be present in the flesh. At that moment, fasting will be appropriate

(5:35). Fasting in this sense is a discipline of longing, mourning the absence of the table and the home for which we were created. This is fasting as a mode of supplication, a type of prayer for the full realization of the Jubilee mission. Jesus himself will fast in just this way. There are other purposes of fasting; we will take up at least one other important purpose later when we discuss the Last Supper.

Jesus does *not* say that, in his bodily absence, his disciples will *only* fast. Rather, he says that *only then* will they fast. Jesus, the bridegroom, is absent in the flesh. The world is not as it should be. The kingdom is not yet. The Jubilee mission is far from complete. So we fast. But Jesus the bridegroom is also present through the Spirit of the living Christ among us. The kingdom is coming; the world is being reformed and transformed. The Jubilee mission continues in our midst. So, like the disciples, we feast. We share meals that are meant to be partial enactments of the eschatological banquet. In this respect, the table fellowship of Jesus and his disciples is very much a model for us.

———

The next meal in Luke is perhaps all too familiar to us: it's a snack on the go. In Luke 6:1-5, Jesus and his disciples are on the move on the Sabbath. As they're walking through grainfields, "his disciples plucked some heads of grain, rubbed them in their hands, and ate them" (6:1).

As they take and eat, the disciples aren't violating anyone's property rights. This precise practice is allowed in the Torah. The provision of plucking heads of grain in Deuteronomy 23:25 comes in the context of supporting the needy.

Even more, what Deuteronomy proposes is a set of practices for recognizing that, despite the human labor involved in the cultivation of grain (and grapes), the fruit of the land, like the land itself, is fundamentally the gift of God. It is no accident, then, that the restrictions put in place to prevent exploitation of Deuteronomy's generous provisions for the poor take the form of the restrictions placed on *manna* in the desert: eat as many grapes as you like, but you cannot keep any extra for tomorrow (Deut 23:24). You may pluck grains by hand as Jesus and his disciples are doing, but you may not use a sickle.

The effect is to recognize even in the cultivated land the nature of it as a gift from God, to recognize it as the land flowing with milk and honey. Describing the land this way, Jan Assmann reminds us, is to emphasize not just the abundant fertility of the land but also the extent to which the land might yield its fruit without the intervention of human labor (124). That is, it is to relate to the land as one should in the year of Jubilee, receiving "what the field itself produces," while the land itself is given a Sabbath rest (Lev 25:12). Bread comes from the mouth of the Lord. In particular, bread comes from the land the Lord has provided to Israel by the promise that issued from God's mouth. The produce of these fields is in some regards like manna in the desert. By whomever they are stewarded—as is particularly plain in *Judea* of all places, even more so in the frame of Jubilee—these are the *Lord's* fields.

All fields, of course, are the Lord's fields. From them comes a bounty that, when we eat of it, draws us into relationship with God through relationship to the fields that

God has created. This relationship is equally available to all—rich and poor, because it recognizes all goods as divine *gifts* rather than mere private property.

In this way, bread becomes an invitation to be at home in the fields, to be at home in the land God has given. This home is *particular* to the particular fields. Where the fields grow wheat, we eat wheat bread. Where the fields grow barley, we eat barley bread (as Jesus and his disciples likely did). Where the fields yield nothing with which to make bread, we don't eat bread at all. Sometimes the "bread" we eat is rice. Global networks of exchange may aid in our forgetting that bread is not just relationship to God through God's creation but rather the relationship to God and to one another through relationships to particular geographies. But, in reality, all bread comes from *somewhere*. When we eat, we are invited to be not just at home with God but at home with God and with particular fields, lakes, pastures, and seas. As the disciples walk and eat of the fruit of the fields in the ways Deuteronomy 23 proposes, they are deeply at home with God in the land God has provided.

In wealthy societies in our globalized world, we are only recently beginning to *notice* that nine or ten or twelve months out of the year much of our produce comes from thousands of miles away. Perhaps, as we begin to take note, we recognize this bizarre fact as evidence of our wealth, privilege, and therefore particular responsibility—and rightly so. Perhaps we begin to consider the ways these habits of eating diminish geographies near and far—and rightly so. Perhaps we can begin to consider how our habits of eating diminish the lives of those unseen who labor over our food in fields unknown. But do we recognize that, as we are alienated from the land that yields our food and the people who labor over it, our own humanity is diminished? Do we recognize that we ourselves are alienated from the rich invitation God has extended to us to be at *home* with God, the land, and the people who share land with us?

————

This transformed relationship with the land and its fruits is what Jesus and his disciples are performing as they snack their way through the fields. But this is not the issue at hand. The issue, as it is on multiple occasions in the Gospel (cf. 6:6-11, 13:10-17, 14:1-6), is whether what Jesus and his disciples are doing is lawful on the Sabbath. "Harvesting" on the Sabbath is forbidden by Exodus 34:21. The question is whether what Jesus and his disciples are doing is harvesting—whether it is Sabbath-violating *work*.

Now, there are several lines of defense available to Jesus. For one, there is the case to be made that, as described above, inasmuch as the provision of Deuteronomy 23:24 invites one to relate to the land as producing of itself, plucking grain is precisely not *work* that would violate the Sabbath. This line of argument would only be deepened if we think in terms of Jubilee and the way the Sabbath rest for the land invites us to relate to it as producing of itself.

More important, perhaps, is the position in which the Pharisees' ruling might leave the poor. In the provision of manna, there was an exception carved out for the Sabbath. You could never collect more than you needed for a day—except on the eve of the Sabbath, when you could collect enough for the Sabbath as well. Only on that night would stockpiled manna not spoil (Exod 16:22-30). The Sabbath laws of the Pharisees, interpreting even plucking by hand as "harvesting," allowed for no such exception. One means the poor had to address their hunger was unavailable on the Sabbath, and there were no provisions for collecting extra the day before. Just how strictly all of these rules were followed—just how directly Deuteronomy's allowances *actually* provided a social safety net in first-century Judea—is beside the point. Rather, the fact is that the conceptual structure marks religious virtue as a luxury good available only to the wealthy. It is not hard to find examples in our day: electric cars, fair-trade clothing, organic food, and sparkling new LEED-certified buildings make it plain that, for us as well, the appearance of virtue is perhaps our most sought-after luxury good. Surely God's law would not similarly make virtue the exclusive property of the wealthy.

In short, Jesus is defending the rights of the poor to sustenance—Sabbath or not. Just a few verses later, Jesus defends his right to heal on the Sabbath with the question: "Is it lawful to do good or to do harm on the sabbath, to save life or to destroy it?" (6:9) As a summary statement at the end of these two Sabbath controversies, and as the first instance of what becomes Jesus' refrain in his teaching on the Sabbath (cf. 13:15, 14:5), we can understand this rhetorical question as speaking also to our controversy about the field snack. The disciples are hungry. Hunger is to be honored. The hungry have the right to sustenance, which

God has provided through creation and, more specifically, through right relationship with each particular land in which human communities find themselves. Jesus, the Lord of the Sabbath (6:5), is honoring the human on the Sabbath in honoring human hunger.

———

Jesus and his disciples are *at home* with God and with one another as they are at home in the fields God has provided and that are to enjoy the Jubilee that God has anointed Jesus to declare. Jesus honors human hunger in his response to the Pharisees' objection. But none of this is explicitly what Jesus *says* when he responds to the accusation from the Pharisees that what he and the disciples are doing is unlawful. Rather, Jesus invokes a story from Hebrew scriptures. And, as in his earlier confrontation with the devil, the small piece he cites perhaps speaks less than the larger context he invokes.

"Have you not read…" (6:3). Surely, this would be received as an insult by his Pharisee interlocutors. They have read the scripture. They have read *every* scripture, over and over. But, time and again in Luke's Gospel, the scriptures are not self-interpreting. Especially when it comes to understanding what they say about Jesus the Messiah, they require eyes that can see and a mind that is open. In the end, they require Jesus himself explaining their meaning (24:27, 45).

At one level, what follows is Jesus citing a rather obscure bit of legal precedent. You think harvesting a few grains by hand and thus breaking Sabbath is bad? Consider what David and his companions did. Hungry and without provisions, they "entered the house of God and took and ate the bread of the Presence, which it is not lawful for any but the priests to eat" (6:4). If the rules governing the bread of the Presence can be bent in order to honor human hunger, how much more a contestable interpretation of the Sabbath laws concerning harvesting?

But there is more going on than establishing a(n admittedly flimsy) legal precedent. The story recalls and deepens the typological relationship already established between these two "anointed ones," David and Jesus. In the infancy narratives, it is noted that Joseph is of the house of David (1:27, 3:31), and the angel Gabriel foretells that Jesus will receive David's throne (1:32). Zechariah, too, invokes David's name (1:69). Bethlehem, the site of Jesus' birth, is twice described as the city of David (2:4, 11). After this invocation of David in chapter 6, David is invoked two more times: once when a blind man calls Jesus "Jesus, Son of David" (18:38), and then later in a midrashic riddle about the Messiah's Davidic identity that Jesus poses to the scribes (20:41-44). While this particular controversy appears in all three synoptic Gospels, the Davidic comparison taps into a particularly deep set of resonances within Luke's Gospel; David is a key reference point for Luke's account of Jesus' messianic identity.

The import of Jesus selecting *this* story from the life of David is that it helps us "sync up the clocks" of the Jesus and David narratives. This story comes from that long period of David's life between his anointing in 1 Samuel 16 and his enthronement after the death of Saul in 2 Samuel 2. In the years in between, David slays Goliath (1 Sam 17) and fights the Philistines (1 Sam 23) and Amalekites (1 Sam 30). These military exploits against the enemies of the people built the legend that would drive Saul's homicidal madness: "Saul has killed his thousands, and David his ten thousands" (1 Sam 18:7-8, 21:11, 29:5).

In short, invoking *this* story from David's life identifies Jesus not just as the Messiah (literally, "the anointed one") but as the anointed-but-not-yet-enthroned one. He is like David; but even more, in his ministry, he is like David in that in-between period between the anointing and the enthronement. Like David in this period, Jesus travels the Judean countryside, rescuing the people from their enemies—in Jesus' case, unclean spirits and illnesses. This is the substance of Jesus' Jubilee mission: casting out an unclean spirit (4:31-37), healing many in Capernaum (4:38-44), cleansing a leper (5:12-16), healing a paralytic (5:17-26). Jesus is proclaiming and effecting *release* of the land and its inhabitants.

It is not hard to map the entirety of the ministry of Jesus onto the life of David. Like David, Jesus is anointed and receives the Spirit well before he is enthroned (3:21-22; cf. 1 Sam 16:1-13). Like David, he does battle against the enemies of the people of Judea (miracles; cf. David's battles against the Philistines). As in David's case, the gap between Jesus' anointing and enthronement invites comparison to the established authorities: the scribes, Pharisees, and Sadducees in Jesus' case, Saul in David's case. As a result, these authorities try to have him killed, just as Saul makes multiple attempts on David's life. Both make triumphant entries into Jerusalem.

Both David and Jesus are eventually enthroned, a fact that forms the basis of the Davidic identification in early Christianity, especially through the invocation of Psalm 110:1: "The LORD says to my Lord, 'Sit at my right hand until I make your enemies your footstool.'" (This Psalm is quoted in Luke 20:42-43; cf. Matt 22:44; Mark 12:36; 1 Cor 15:25; Acts 2:34; Heb 1:13.) Doubtless, this psalm is again in mind when Jesus declares at his trial, "But from now on the Son of Man will be seated at the right hand of the power of God" (22:69). This final invocation of the psalm in Luke speaks to the central mystery of his messiahship: namely, that he is enthroned only after his death and resurrection—and even then, only in the heavenly realm (Acts 7:55-56). The time of his full enthronement awaits that time when he will eat the feast of the kingdom anew in a world renewed (Luke 22:16-18). Only then will Gabriel's prophecy from Luke 1 be fulfilled: "He will reign over the house of Jacob forever, and of his kingdom there will be no end" (1:33).

Luke invokes this whole trajectory of the life of David as a key lens through which to understand Jesus as Messiah. But here in Luke 6:1-5, he invites us to understand Jesus' earthly ministry in light of the anointed-but-not-yet-enthroned David, liberating the people of God from their enemies—but not yet fully calling the shots. This adds a new layer of resonance to Jesus' Jubilee mission statement, declared through citation of the prophet Isaiah in Luke 4:18-19.

The Spirit is upon Jesus to set the people free. But we shouldn't move too quickly past this fact: the land and the people in it *need* a Jubilee. Not all is well. And it is not because Jesus, the king, has fallen asleep on the job. It is because Jesus *is not yet enthroned.* The kingdom has not yet come (even if it is "at hand"); this is why we ought to pray for it to come (Luke 11:2). This is no small mystery—so we ought to be careful lest we say more than we ought to dare—but the picture the synoptic Gospels paint of Jesus is not one of the puppet master of the universe come briefly to play a part (even a central role) on the stage of the puppet theater. Rather, the picture is of a rightful king come to liberate a land under the unjust and destructive rule of a usurper. God may be sovereign over all, but, on the "micro" scale of the times in which he and we live, Jesus leads a nonviolent righteous *insurrection.* And he empowers and authorizes his followers to enter into his Jubilee work (10:1-24).

As David chases the enemies of the people of God from the land, so, too, Jesus travels about liberating the Judean countryside. As he insists, his ministry extends beyond Judea (4:23-30), but it begins with Judea, with securing the land against God's enemies. It begins with preparing the land, preparing the *fields* for the banquet of the kingdom.

——

To say that Jesus, as Messiah, is like David is no great insight. The word, "Messiah," itself *means* "anointed." David is the anointed one par excellence. The puzzle is what *sort* of Davidic king. Davidic in what sense? *King* in what sense? The occasion of the plucking of wheat in the fields provides an opening to "sync" the stories of Jesus the Messiah and David the anointed-but-not-yet-enthroned king of Israel, offering a point of leverage for wrestling with this Messianic puzzle.

But, as we saw in the cases of Elijah, Elisha, and Moses in the feeding of the 5,000, so here: Jesus is *more* than David. Once again, the hermeneutical key is the word "lord." After briefly retelling the story of David and his companions' eating of the bread of the Presence, Jesus concludes: "The Son of Man is lord of the sabbath" (6:5). The Greek draws our attention to this word, *kurios*, "Lord." "Lord he is of the sabbath, the Son of Man," an unduly wooden translation might go. Jesus claims to be lord of the Sabbath. The phrase invokes the Torah's typical invocation of Sabbath as "a sabbath for the Lord," where *kurios* in the Greek translation of the Hebrew Bible is translating "Yahweh," the unspeakable "proper name" of God (e.g., Exod 16:23, 25; 20:10; Lev 23:3; Deut 5:14). (All of the passages we have already referenced about Sabbath practice—from the Sabbath for the land to the Jubilee to the manna exception—use this phrase.) Jesus is not merely claiming to be lord of the interpretation of Sabbath rules. He is claiming to be the Lord *for whom* and *to whom* the Sabbath is celebrated.

To identify Jesus this way is not to contradict his identity as the Davidic Messiah but to begin to understand the meaning of that title. As Jesus later riddles the scribes:

> How can they say that the Messiah is David's son? For David himself says in the book of Psalms, "The Lord said to my Lord, 'Sit at my right hand, until I make your

enemies your footstool.'" David thus calls him Lord; so
how can he be his son? (20:41-44)

Having already fallen silent after the previous exchange
(20:40), the scribes are unwilling to offer a response. But
those with ears to hear can perhaps dare to wonder: Is this
One whom David calls Lord in fact *the* Lord, *kurios*, *Yahweh*,
the God of Israel? Could this be who Jesus is claiming to
be? Perhaps Jesus is entitled to the bread of the presence
because it is the bread of *his* presence. Perhaps the bread of
his presence is out in the fields because his presence is out
in the fields. If so, have we recognized his presence there?
Have we sought the Divine presence in the fields and wilds
whence the food on our tables comes?

———

Even now, Jesus is as he has taught us: anointed but not
yet finally enthroned. The banquet to which we are invited
beckons from the future of the advent of God. In the mean-
time, Jesus invites us to walk the fields in his presence and
receive the goodness of God's gifts. He invites us to enter
into his Jubilee work, liberating the land: driving out the
illnesses, hunger, unjust structures, and evil powers that
hold the land in captivity. He invites us to eat the fruit of
the fields in ways that constitute homes that are sites of
intimacy among God, people, and places. He invites us to
hope for that day in which we may eat of the banquet of the
kingdom among fields, lakes, forests, rivers, pastures, and
seas at home in having become the home of God.

DISCUSSION QUESTIONS

1. What would Jesus' declaration of Jubilee mean for your neighborhood or your city? How is Jesus inviting you to participate in his mission of Jubilee?

2. How can we eat in ways that help us to be mindful of the places from which our food comes?

3. Jesus honors hunger. How is Jesus inviting you to honor the hunger of those around you?

4. In what ways is it helpful to think about Jesus as anointed-but-not-yet-enthroned? In what ways is it troubling?

PRAYER

Lord of the Jubilee, capture our hearts with Your vision of rest and release for our lands and for our neighbors. Lord of the harvest, make us mindful of Your provision and through whose hands and whose land it comes. Son of David, have mercy on us. Set us free. Amen.

3

Sinners at the Table

Luke 5:27-32, 7:36-50, 15:11-32

Often, when we think about who is invited to the table, whom *others* invite, who *always* seems to have a seat at the table, we worry about who is being excluded. We call one another out for who's left out. It's the chief sin of our contemporary world: unfair exclusion. Jesus got in trouble for the opposite: he got in trouble for who was *welcomed*. No one was excluded—which was itself the problem. (Perhaps especially in moments of increased political polarization like ours, we, too, can relate to this sort of "problem": welcoming the wrong sorts of people can appear to be a failure to recognize the demands of justice.) Ironically, one common way to end up on the outside of Jesus' invitation was to refuse the irrelevance of qualifications for presence at the table. And, still, Jesus would come on over for dinner. Even those who excluded themselves could do no more than *imagine* themselves "outside" the feast in the midst of a meal where Jesus was inviting them to the banquet of the kingdom Jubilee.

———

It all begins when Levi, the tax collector, catches Jesus' eye (5:27). We have already discussed the specter of the tax man's reach in Roman Palestine when we noted Simon's likely situation as a fisherman on the Sea of Galilee. As with the lake, so, too, with so many other aspects of daily life: taxes were collected when you crossed borders and bridges and when you arrived in harbors and as you entered significant cities. But we must understand, tax collectors were not governmental bureaucrats; the Romans had turned over tax collection to private enterprise. Tax collectors leased the right to collect taxes in one or another place or on one or another set of goods and then would extract as much as they could in order to pay for the lease of taxing rights and turn a handsome profit. This model was reproduced at multiple levels of subleasing. The one selling the lease got guaranteed income; the one buying it gained whatever excess he believed he could get over the cost of the lease. Levi was a "tax farmer," extracting whatever he could to pay off his contract and turn a profit, mediating the foreign rule of Caesar while enriching himself. He was a traitor and a crook all wrapped in one.

It is this man, this *tax collector*, to whom Jesus issues his classic invitation: "Follow me" (5:27). Levi, leaving everything, gets up and follows Jesus (v. 28).

This invitation to discipleship may have been enough to cause offense to those troubled by the way Levi made a living, but there is no offense reported until Jesus is spotted *eating* with Levi and his friends. Levi's first act of discipleship is to throw a banquet for Jesus in his home. This is no small thing. After all, a first-century Palestinian meal was an intimate affair: the ceremonial ablutions, the kiss of greeting, reclining at the table. When we imagine Levi and his friends celebrating with Jesus, we should imagine they are leaning up against one another and embracing; this is part of what it meant to share a meal. This draws the ire of the Pharisees, who complain to Jesus' disciples: "Why do you eat and drink with tax collectors and sinners?" (5:30) This is the first, but by no means the last, time in Luke that Jesus' and his disciples' eating habits will be the target of critique (cf. 5:33, 7:31-34). Each time, Luke's point is not that Jesus' critics are getting caught up in trivialities but rather that controversies about Jesus' habits of table fellowship reveal central aspects of Jesus' identity and mission. This instance is no exception.

Despite the Pharisees registering their complaint with the disciples, Jesus answers them directly: "Those who are well have no need of a physician, but those who are sick; I have come to call not the righteous but sinners to repentance" (5:31-32). This is a pillar of Jesus' Jubilee mission: to forgive sins. The preceding passage centers on a controversy about his authority to do just that (5:17-26). There, Jesus proves his authority to forgive a man's sins by healing his body (5:23-24). Here, he explains his predilection for relational intimacy with sinners in terms of a healer's calling to the sick.

To be clear, Jesus does not reject the Pharisees' estimation of Levi and his tax-collecting friends as sinners. He is not advocating that these uptight religious folks chill out. Extracting taxes from the rural poor who could barely afford to live as it was is no small matter. Nor is betraying the people of God and, even more, participating in the empire of Caesar. Jesus' intimacy with Levi and his ilk does not depend on, nor does it amount to, an endorsement of their way of life. On the contrary, Jesus draws near on account of their sin.

In Levi's case, Jesus draws near on account of Levi's *repentance* from sin. Luke 5:28 begins in Greek: "and forsaking all . . ." This turning away from sin is a cause for celebration (Luke 15). It is cause for a great feast. But Levi is not the only one at the table. "There was a large crowd of tax collectors," Luke tells us (5:29). These, presumably, have not (yet?) repented. In their case, Jesus draws near because they are sick and in need of a physician. They are sinners whom he must call, as he has already called Levi.

This banquet is these two things at once: the feast rejoicing over one sinner who repents (Luke 15) and the banquet calling sinners to repent through the visceral experience of extravagant hospitality and the joy of repentance. At its best, our meals ought to be just this: the interweaving of joy over repentance from the injustice and wickedness that make us sick and result from the ongoing illness of our souls and the wooing of the healing presence of the One who can make us well. When our meals can be these two things at once, they are a picture of life together with God—true life in the midst of false life—to which Jesus calls us. It is in this place that we can come to be at home together, to belong to one another, lured by the one who invites us to be at home with him.

———

In Luke 7:36-50, once again, there are two meals happening at once. Simon, a Pharisee, has invited Jesus to eat with him. No doubt, Simon is hopeful this dinner will be of a more savory sort than the party at Levi's house. Like the account of Levi's banquet, this story, too, will become a dinner party about how to give dinner parties. It won't be the last of this type, either.

Simon's hopes for decorum are dashed almost immediately. Just after narrating Jesus taking his place at the table, Luke describes the entry of a woman, a "sinner," who kneels behind Jesus, weeping, bathing his feet with her tears and anointing them with ointment. To call this a breach of protocol is a vast understatement. As a Pharisee, Simon has particular responsibilities in hosting this meal with respect to his and his guests' ritual purity. The woman's presence threatens this purity. (That Simon himself has already failed in his responsibilities as host is a detail Luke saves for later.) Seeing the woman, Simon mutters to himself, "If this man were a prophet, he would have known who and what kind of woman this is who is touching him—that she is a sinner" (7:39). As in the passage above, Jesus answers a concern not shared with him, this time with a parable that demonstrates that he is a prophet who does know this woman touching him is a sinner.

Jesus offering a parable would presumably have pleased Simon. This is the sort of teaching for which Jesus is known. And an open-ended parable would be a delightful way to kick off the meaty part of the symposium conversation. As a parable, this story about different debtors forgiven different sizes of debts fits the bill of framing the dinner and getting it off on good footing. Jesus begins the dialogue with a simple question for his host: Which debtor will love the creditor more? Simon suggests the one with the greater debt; Jesus affirms his correct answer. All seems to be going well.

The whole scene takes a turn when Jesus breaks the abstraction of the parable and turns everyone's attention to the material circumstances around them: "Do you see this woman?" (7:44) This was the question Simon was asking himself about Jesus: Does Jesus *see* this woman? Does he recognize the threat she is to his purity and to the symposium itself? Jesus turns the table. Perhaps it is Simon who cannot see rightly.

But this exchange is more than a contest between two male subjects' ability to rightly assess a female *object*. Through his parable, Jesus has focused attention on the *woman's* ability to assess the worthiness of the one who has forgiven her. Ultimately, seeing her rightly is a matter of recognizing her as perceptive, as one who *really* sees what is on offer in Jesus' Jubilee mission to forgive sins. Forgiven much, she loves much.

We said the whole scene had taken a turn only when Jesus asks Simon his pointed question. In reality, the dinner party had gone off the rails far earlier. Because a meal is more than a *mere* meal, but rather an enactment of a home, the meal began before they came to the table. It began when Jesus had entered Simon's house. And it was in this moment that this would-be home failed *as* a home. Jesus was denied the customary hospitality: he was given no water to wash his feet; Simon did not anoint his head with oil; Simon did not greet him with a kiss. Home, after all, is also enacted through *touch*. The physical intimacy was part of why table fellowship signified so deeply. The meal at Simon's house proves to be profoundly *un-homed* through precisely this lack of hospitality. The woman at Jesus' feet provides the very starkest contrast—a damning critique of Simon's lack of hospitality—and Jesus says as much (7:44-46). By comparison, it is the *woman* who is acting as host. It is she who is in a much more significant sense at home with Jesus, having welcomed him to be at home in her presence.

Jesus' clarification of his mission at the table with Levi's friends defined not only to whom Jesus was called (sinners), but also to whom he was not (the righteous). At first glance, this might seem to exclude a whole category of righteous people from Jesus' mission—perhaps excluding someone precisely like this curious if inhospitable Pharisee, Simon. The parable of the debtors might also seem to draw distinctions between two groups of people who will experience Jesus' ministry differently. Those forgiven much love much. Those forgiven little love little.

But the fact is: Jesus eats with Simon the Pharisee. His exclusive call to sinners does not prevent him from eating with this "righteous" man. The logic is clear: Jesus calls only sinners. Jesus eats with Simon, calling him to life. Therefore, Simon is a sinner. Simon is just as much a target of Jesus' mission—just as much a sick man to whom Jesus the healer has come—as the woman at Jesus' feet. But this is not Simon's experience. Why? This is what the parable is to explain.

Simon is not doomed to love less because he's been forgiven less. If Simon loves less, if he fails to see Jesus as the woman rightly perceives him, it is because he knows himself less as a sinner forgiven. The issue is not Simon's objective status but rather his subjective self-assessment. Jesus' pro-sinner policy does not marginalize Simon. It forces him to come to terms with his status as a sinner. This is what Simon must do. If he can, he is as welcome as he could ever hope to be. If not, Simon, who had invited this "prophet" to come and speak to him, will marginalize himself, placing himself outside the heart of Jesus' mission and outside the move of God in his midst.

———

The parables of lost things in Luke 15—the lost sheep (vv. 4-7), the lost coin (vv. 8-10), and the lost son (vv. 11-32)—are some of the most well-known of Jesus' parables. Told and retold, these parables famously tell of God's love for repentant sinners. Lest we miss the point, each of the first two parables ends with a straightforward statement of the moral of the story: "Just so, I tell you, there will be more joy in heaven over one sinner who repents than over ninety-nine righteous persons who need no repentance" (15:7; cf. 15:10).

These stories are mainstays of Sunday school lessons the world over—and for good reason. But even if we are familiar with them, perhaps we forget that they are told in response to the Pharisees' complaint, "This fellow welcomes sinners and eats with them" (15:2). This famous set of parables is intended to speak to the appropriateness of the celebration at Levi's banquet and the extravagance of gratitude at Simon's dinner party. They are considered theological defenses for hearty feasting, for motley crowds celebrating even just one repentant sinner.

While the first two parables have the most straightforward "morals" attached to them, laying out plainly how they answer the Pharisees' and scribes' critiques, it is the third that most organically weaves together sin, repentance, touch, and table fellowship with sinners as a robust response. The story may be familiar. The younger of two sons asks for his inheritance early, and his father agrees. The son wastes the inheritance and ends up destitute. He takes a job tending to pigs and finds himself so poor, so hungry, that he longs to eat the slop he feeds the pigs.

This is when the pivotal moment comes. Jesus says the son "came to himself" (15:17). The actions that follow from this moment will twice be described by the father as nothing less than a return from the dead (15:24, 32). The son considers his dire straits and the relative comfort of even those who work as wage workers for his father. He resolves to return to his father and confess his sin: "Father, I have sinned against heaven and before you; I am no longer worthy to be called your son; treat me like one of your hired hands" (15:18-19).

Before the son can even make his speech, the father welcomes him, the repentant sinner, with open arms, running to him and kissing him—the kiss Simon did not offer Jesus, the kiss the woman did. When the son finally is able to make his confession, the father responds immediately by declaring a feast, commanding his servants, "'Quickly, bring out a robe—the best one—and put it on him; put a ring on his finger and sandals on his feet. And get the fatted calf and kill it, and let us eat and celebrate; for this son of mine was dead and is alive again; he was lost and is found!' And they began to celebrate" (15:22-24). As Jesus has twice made clear already in the preceding parables, this is simply what you *do* with repentant sinners. Feasting is the proper response to repentance. Because repentance is like the dead being raised back to life. It is the restoration of ruptured relationship. It is a return home. And what better way to mark that than with a joyful feast?

The speed and depth of the father's response might leave an important matter hanging in the air: the younger son's claim to no longer be worthy to be called the father's son. Tellingly, the father refuses even to respond to this absurd suggestion. He welcomes his son *as* his son, ignoring his appeal to be treated as a mere hired hand. As much as his repentance entails an admission of guilt—which, undoubtedly, it does—that guilt does not make the son unworthy of the love of his father. And as central as repentance is—as worthy a cause of celebration as it might be—it does not make the son worthy of the love of his father. He cannot be *made* worthy because he has always been worthy. His worthiness rests in his prior status as son—as a member of the family. He hasn't arrived at a job; he's returned *home*. And the celebratory feast marks that return and performs the very restored at-homeness that is being celebrated, as father and son and other members of the household recline at the table and share in the finest fruits of the land they work together. The feast is no mere *response* to repentance; it is also the very fruit of repentance realized: reconciled relationship, a restored experience of home. If the feast with Levi and his friends was a meal *at home*, shared in the intimacy of mutual belonging, and the meal at Simon's house was a meal *un-homed*, the feast celebrating the return of the prodigal is a meal *re-homed*, a meal that participates in and contributes to the restoration of home where it had been lost.

At this point, this story is only barely a parable. The Pharisees and their scribes take issue with Jesus feasting with sinners. Jesus tells a story about feasting with a sinner. The directness of the parable runs the risk of simply leading to the same disconnect between Jesus and his critics. So, Jesus writes his critics into the story in the form of the elder brother.

The elder brother is concerned about fairness. He has been righteous all these years. He never asked for his share of the inheritance. He never wasted it all. And he never so much as received a goat from his father to celebrate with his friends. He complains to the father: "But when this son of yours came back, who has devoured your property with prostitutes, you killed the fatted calf for him!" (15:30).

The elder brother is the perfect stand-in for the Pharisees. He sees the feast as a waste: a waste of resources and a waste of honor bestowed and celebration received. He considers himself righteous and therefore unfairly excluded from the wastefully (one might say prodigally) extravagant embrace of the father. If this is who Jesus is—or who Jesus thinks God is—then they resonate with the elder son's rejection of the "goodness" of this father.

The younger son's sin is quite serious. At its root is a profound rejection of intimacy with the father and with the father's home. When the younger son asks for his inheritance, he wishes his father dead and reduces his relationship with his father to a wealth-transfer mechanism. He reduces his relationship with his brother to a competition for the father's goods, settled as a draw. He reduces the land and what they had made of it to mere property—land that is no more than land. Were the feast a sign that the father didn't recognize this harm or, worse, endorsed it, the elder son's indignance would be justified. But it is clear from the story that the father recognizes the younger son's sin. By the father's account, having wished his father dead, severed his relationship to his home, and wasted his inheritance in a sinful way of life, the younger son was *dead*. The father's feast is not evidence of him failing to take the son's sin seriously; it is evidence of just how seriously he takes it and therefore how great a cause for joy his repentance is. This is important for the Pharisees' critique. Jesus' eating habits do not mean he's a libertine, glutton, and drunk (7:34).

In reality, the elder son is also lost. He has not rejected the father's home but rather has developed deep attachment to an *un-homed* image of home. The elder son is quite attached to the land and the animals. This is why the concerns for fairness come rushing so quickly to the fore when he hears the father is killing the fatted calf. As heir to the share of the estate that is left, that calf belongs to the elder son. This is all the elder son hears when the father assures him: "all that is mine is yours" (15:31). That is, he, too, effectively wishes the father dead and reduces the father to wealth transfer. What he cannot hear is the true nature of mutuality and belonging to the father's home contained in this affirmation. Because the elder son has no appreciation of the father's role and the father's grace as the foundation of the entire order of the home, he does not appreciate that the invitation to share in all that is the father's is an invitation to be at home with the father and with all who are at home with the father.

As a result, the elder son doesn't understand what "ownership" means within the home, among those who belong to one another in it. To "own" is not to exercise sovereign rights of disposal. Rather, it is to have certain rights and responsibilities of *use*. And, within the home, among those responsibilities is the responsibility to use what we have for the sake of love—to build and maintain the home as a home of *love*. From this point of view, what better use is there than to celebrate this resurrection of the lost son? None of this makes any sense to the elder son because he does not understand the nature of the father's home and the abundance of life within it.

As the parable ends, the possibility of this celebratory feast becoming the enactment of home it is intended to be lies in the balance. It depends on the elder son. Will he repent of his sin? Will he turn from instrumentalization of family and home to the genuine embrace of the father? Will we?

———

As our colleague Linn Tonstad writes,

> The shape of Christian existence is celebration of the presence of Christ at a banquet. The promise of Christian existence is that banquets without borders express the victorious truth of human existence. Equally, the shape of Christian conflict is over who gets to participate in that celebration and under what conditions. (239)

These passages in Luke lead us headlong into this conflict, by naming a number of different types of sinners—that is, a number of different ways sin may be perceived. There are those "obvious" sinners, "moral failures" of the sort Simon takes the woman at his house to represent. Jesus welcoming these folks offends our moral and religious sensibilities, our intuitions that we ought to preserve a moral purity of some sort—for our sake, for our children's sake, what have you.

Then there are those who, like the tax collectors, have failed the justice test. Perhaps these are folks we recognize as our political enemies, not just in the sense that they "root for the other team," but in ways that we insist demonstrate some deep moral failure in the public realm. The more we unveil the political and economic systems around us, the deeper our sense of these folks' moral failure becomes. Perhaps we are even correct in some of our assessments of these systems and the roles played by various "sinners" of this sort. Jesus drawing near to these people offends our political purity, our patriotism, our desire only to affiliate—and for Jesus only to affiliate—with those "on the right side of history."

Then there are those we view as being like the Pharisees, those who sit in judgment of others' moral failings and see themselves as above reproach. We try not to notice that, in distancing ourselves from them, we do exactly what we are singling out for judgment. Perhaps our biblical imagination is distorted enough to imagine that Jesus simply *does not* draw near to these folks. These people, we imagine, are Jesus' enemies, plain and simple. But, again and again in the Gospels, Jesus engages these religious folks. He dialogues with them, gifts them a good argument, if that's what the moment requires. He even goes to dinner with them.

Most difficult of all, perhaps, are those sinners we experience as having harmed us in the intimate realm of *family*. A child who has betrayed us. A sibling who thinks only of himself or loves to smugly look down his nose on us. Small slights, repeated over years, leave deep wounds. In relationships with this sort of depth, we believe we've learned how to read between the lines, see what's behind the curtain, and assess what's been swept under the rug. We can see the convoluted self-deceptions and recurring cycles of harm. And we're not wrong—at least almost never entirely. The father's embrace of the prodigal offends something deep within us that brings together every type of resentment we've cataloged thus far. But he kills the fatted calf. And invites us to celebrate and to celebrate with *them*.

Rather than choose among these sinners or rank their impurity, Jesus invites them all to the table. He invites them to experience themselves at home in one another's presence. He invites them to be at home in his transforming, forgiving presence. This is Jesus' posture toward us as well. Coming to the table requires admitting that we are "qualified" for membership as sinners and, before that, children. But coming to the table isn't just a matter of coming to understand our status before Jesus as one of his patients in need of healing. Coming to know ourselves as sinners may be easier than coming to know ourselves as sinners like *them*, as *their* family. Receiving forgiveness may be easier than being forgiven alongside *them*, coming to know ourselves as belonging to one another. This is an important component of the kingdom work being done at Jesus' table. As a *table*, this site of repentance, of forgiveness, and of celebration is a site of *fellowship* among sinners. With the table as the goal, we begin to see the ways that repenting and extending forgiveness are interwoven as habits of reconciliation. In these meals, should we accept the invitation to the table, we find ourselves not just at home with the one who calls us to the table but at home with those whom he has called home. And as we enter into this shared joy at experiencing Jubilee release, the joy itself binds us together and begins to open to us a picture of what it would mean to be at home with one another in a world made the home of God.

Those steeped in certain sorts of Christian practice will be quick to think here of the liturgical feast, the Eucharist. Without a doubt, we are invited to this table in the sacrament of the Lord's Supper. But, as we have seen, this is by no means the only meal Jesus eats. And it is not the only table to which he invites sinners to come and be at home with him and with one another. Rather, this "Jubilee meal," this banquet of sinners called to repentance, celebrating repentance, and beginning a new life at home with one another, speaks to a latent possibility for all of our meals, should we choose to eat while being mindful of doing so in the presence of Christ Jesus.

DISCUSSION QUESTIONS

1. What feelings arise for you when you think of Jesus relating to you as a sinner called to repentance?

2. Whose sin do you find it hardest to forgive? What sort of sin are you uncomfortable thinking of as being in any sense *like* yours? Whose presence at Jesus' table do you find troubling?

3. What would it look like for *all* of our meals to be opportunities for Jesus to do his work of inviting all us sinners to repentance, celebrating repentance with us, and inviting us to be at home with him and with one another?

4. In light of these stories from Jesus' life, who might God be challenging you to invite to share a meal?

PRAYER

All that we have seen thus far is summarized in the Lord's Prayer as recorded by Luke (11:2-4):

"Father, hallowed be your name. Your kingdom come."
Holy Father God, let the Jubilee of our anointed-and-soon-to-be-enthroned Messiah come to be in our world.

"Give us each day our daily bread."
Give us bread that is more than mere bread, but bread that invites us to be at home with our heavenly Father, with the fields and lakes God created, and with one another.

"And forgive us our sins, for we ourselves forgive everyone indebted to us."
Invite us to that table where all of us sinners eat side by side, forgiving and forgiven.

"And do not bring us to the time of trial."
Spare us trial, but, even then, we are ready to say: we do not live by bread alone, but by every word which comes from Jesus our Lord.

4

Rich and Poor at the Table

Luke 14:1-24, 16:1-31

In Jesus' announcement of his ministry, he slips a part of a verse from Isaiah 58 into the midst of a recitation of Isaiah 61. He declares: "The Spirit of the Lord is upon me because he has anointed me . . . to let the oppressed go free . . ." (Luke 4:18). If, taking our cue, we continue the recitation, we respond, "to share your bread with the hungry, and bring the homeless poor into your house . . . not to hide yourself from your own kin" (Isa 58:7). This, too, is the substance of Jesus' Jubilee mission, the definition of *true fasting* (Isa 58:6) that his *feasting* enacts: sharing bread with the hungry and welcoming the unhoused into houses, recognizing in them our family, members of our household. The accounts of Jesus' meals in Luke bear out this purpose:

meals are to be opportunities for rich and poor to be at home with one another.

———

It's striking what Jesus notes about the many meals he eats in Luke, especially compared to what the world's rich tend to focus on in our gastronomic adventures. We fastidiously document the *food*, creating social media posts of beautifully plated courses. We eagerly share with one another news of a great food truck, supermarket find, or recipe. However, as a meal fades further from memory, an interesting shift takes place. When we regale one another with stories of great meals, we may describe the food, but we may say just as much about the moment, the setting, and, perhaps most of all, the people present to share it with us. Jesus begins where we finish, and he does so with a richer set of concerns born of richer aspirations.

Coming from our food-obsessed moment, reading Jesus' speeches at these meals can be akin to the first time you encounter a restaurant or shop obsessed with *presentation*—how food *looks*. Surely, you think to yourself, they're missing the point. Jesus hardly says a word about the food or the wine. There's not a single comment that could count as a culinary insight. His comments are about foot-washing, greeting kisses at the door, seating charts, invitation lists, and who gets invited back. He is consistently concerned with who is at the table and how they are relating to one another. His primary concern is with hospitality, how a meal functions as a focal site of literal home-making, how a group of people find themselves at home with one another and with God through the preparation and eating of a meal.

In Luke 14, Jesus is again eating in the home of a Pharisee. He's been invited for Shabbat dinner. Confronted with a man with acute swelling, Jesus readily receives the interruption and heals the man. He does not let either Sabbath or a meal stand in the way of caring for this man in his need. There is no neat sequestering of times. There is no Sabbath time or meal time, no "I've just sat down to eat and it's 'me' time," or "we've just gathered and it's 'us' time." As throughout his ministry, Jesus is prepared to be interrupted by one in need, prepared to reconceive the "us" for whom this time is reserved. He offers this urgency of need as his defense for healing on the Sabbath (14:5), and the meal begins.

Seeing the way the guests at the meal are jockeying for position around the table, Jesus launches into a teaching about seating charts. Rather than talk directly about Shabbat dinner, he talks about a wedding feast. This is a rather thin veil to draw over his critique of his tablemates. More likely, the point is to invoke the image of the eschatological wedding feast (e.g., Isa 61:10, hinted at through Jesus' recitation of Isa 61:1-2 in Luke 4), which is always lurking behind these discussions of meals and explicitly comes into view in 14:14. But the advice has practical consequences in the here and now: don't elbow your way to the best seat, lest you overestimate your importance and be humiliated when you have to move your way down the table. Rather, take a low seat and you will be honored when the host invites you to move up.

Having given his review of his tablemates, Jesus turns his attention to his host. He's gotten the invitation list all wrong. Rather than inviting those who can return the favor, he should be inviting "the poor, the crippled, the lame, and the blind" (14:13). Having invited the wealthy, they are liable to invite him back. Having been paid back, he'll have forfeited a more valuable repayment in the world to come. As in 6:35-36, the world to come is here imagined as a world of recompense for that which cannot be repaid in this life. Living for rewards in this life amounts to robbing oneself of rewards in the consummated kingdom. Furthermore, inasmuch as giving without expecting return marks people as "children of the Most High" who give without expecting return (6:35), seeking recompense robs folks of an identity that could be theirs even now. In any case, the prospect of repaid hospitality in the world to come looms large over an important strand of Luke's reflection about relationships between rich and poor.

Picking up on Jesus' invocation of this motif of the eschatological banquet, one of his tablemates interjects: "Blessed is anyone who will eat bread in the kingdom of God!" (14:15). This enigmatic response tees up Jesus for a parable that aims to convey something about the connection between our table practices here and now and that final banquet to come.

In the parable, a wealthy householder decides to throw a "great dinner." We know the host is wealthy because he commands servants and is routinely described as a "lord" and as the "house master." His invitation list runs entirely counter to Jesus' advice given just a moment ago.

He invites his social peers or, perhaps, social betters, hoping to use the dinner as an opportunity to accrue social capital. But each begins making excuses: one cannot come because he has bought a piece of land, another because he has just purchased oxen, another because he was recently married. Each excuse is evidence of the social status of the invitees—that they have the means to buy land, to purchase new livestock, to take leave of their social duties when newly married. Jesus' audience would easily have recognized the shame experienced by the householder as, one by one, each of his invitees turns him down. The strategy to build social capital has backfired. The dinner is becoming an embarrassment.

All this would have been familiar, even painfully so. But then the house master does something unexpected. Angry, he sends his servant to recruit a new batch of guests: the poor, the crippled, and the lame (14:21)—that is, the invitation list Jesus had just recommended. When all these are gathered and the house is still not full, he sends the servant out again to cast the search yet wider. "For I tell you," warns the master, "none of those who were invited will taste my dinner" (14:24).

It is tempting to read this parable as an allegory: the master is God, the banquet is the feast of the kingdom Jesus' interlocutor mentioned in 14:15, and the various groups of guests are the various would-be guests at the eschatological banquet. But Jesus' parables are rarely straightforward allegories—and this one in particular presents serious theological challenges if read allegorically. As Joel Green notes, on the allegorical reading, God's original preference in dinner guests would be like our worst impulses. God would prefer the wealthy and influential; the poor would be God's guests of last resort (556). This would run counter to the heart of God as depicted in Luke's Gospel (6:35-36).

The more reasonable approach is to leave the parable in the realm of our hospitality practices in the here and now. In this sense, the parable is a more elaborate depiction of the sort of hypothetical Jesus proposed in 14:8-11. This time, the scenario is depicted from the point of view of the host rather than the guests. Like the guests in the original scenario, this host overestimates his social status and suffers shame. The takeaway is the same: don't play the honor game; it's too risky. The surer bet is to practice hospitality, to leverage your house, if you are fortunate enough to steward one, in ways that store up reward in a different realm. This parable has implications for the feast of the kingdom, but we have to read further to tease those out.

———

In Luke 16:19-31, Jesus tells another parable about feasting. Strikingly, however, this nameless rich man's feasts were not an *occasion* like the celebration of the return of the lost son in chapter 15 or even the social scheming of the host in chapter 14, but rather a way of life: he "feasted sumptuously every day" (v. 19). As Joel Green notes, this depiction may have called to mind for Jesus' hearers legends about King Agrippa II, who was said to host daily feasts (605). There is no mention of guests at this rich man's table. While the depiction of his house as having gates invites us to imagine an extensive household, within the scope of the parable, the rich man feasts alone, dressed in purple and fine linen. This is a parody of what we have learned thus far of the value of meals. These meals are un-homed, even un-homing.

The weight of this alienating eating falls, predictably if infuriatingly, on the poor. Outside the rich man's gates lies a poor man whom, unlike the rich man, Jesus names: Lazarus (16:20). The naming of the poor man alongside a nameless rich man is a clue inviting us to expect a reversal of fortunes. Nevertheless, at first, Lazarus' condition is wretched. Like the prodigal in Luke 15, Lazarus is so poor that he longs to eat what is destined for animals. The dogs who eat the scraps from the rich man's table are in an advantageous position compared to Lazarus; they care for *his* sores (16:21). If we hold a memory of the scene at Simon the Pharisee's house in mind, the touch of these dogs' tongues on Lazarus' sores appear as damning indictments of the rich man's inhospitality toward Lazarus, as the woman's tears were an indictment of Simon's inhospitality toward Jesus.

Following so closely on the parable of the prodigal, it's tempting to embed this parable inside that one, as if this were the story of the prodigal so mistreated by the pig farmer that he longed to eat the pig slop. What became of that rich man who was so callous toward the lost son? In a way (not that these two stories are strictly harmonizable), here Jesus tells the other side of this earlier story.

Both Lazarus and the rich man die. The poor man, as we might expect from consulting our own actuarial tables, dies first. The rich man finds himself tormented in Hades, while Lazarus has been carried by angels to the bosom of Abraham. Here we have a fulfillment of the eschatological reversals hymned in the Magnificat ("he has filled the hungry with good things, and sent the rich away empty," 1:53) and predicted in Luke 6: "Blessed are you who are poor, for yours is the kingdom of God. Blessed are you who are hungry now, for you will be filled. . . . But woe to you who are rich, for you have received your consolation. Woe to you who are full now, for you will be hungry" (vv. 20-21, 24-25). Abraham confirms as much in the parable itself, addressing the rich man: "Child, remember that during your lifetime you received your good things, and Lazarus in like manner evil things; but now he is comforted here, and you are in agony" (16:25). There may be some tenderness in Abraham calling him "child," an expression of compassion for the rich man as a wrongdoer. But surely the words of John the Baptist from Luke 3:8 are to ring in our ears: "Bear fruits worthy of repentance. Do not begin to say to yourselves, 'We have Abraham as our father'; for I tell you, God is able from these stones to raise up children to Abraham." The rich man is a child of Abraham; this is not in dispute. The issue is whether he has repented and borne fruits worthy of repentance.

Seeing Lazarus in the distance with Abraham, the rich man proposes two solutions to his predicament. First, he asks Abraham to send Lazarus to bring him even a drop of water (v. 24), but Abraham replies that it is impossible (v. 26). Second, he asks Abraham to send Lazarus to his brothers lest they suffer this same fate. Abraham insists it is no use. With each request, the rich man only deepens his profound alienation from Lazarus, who remains for him only an errand boy to do his bidding. The contrast between this deep estrangement between Lazarus and the rich man, on the one hand, and the intimacy between Lazarus and Abraham, on the other, could not be sharper. The touch the rich man denied and the dogs supplied to his shame, Abraham now offers. It is now the rich man who is inaccessible to physical touch, perhaps an appropriate fate for one who wished to dine alone dressed in splendor.

———

This is not how it should have been. Jesus' Jubilee declaration does not aim at inflicting the satiated with hunger; the goal is not to punish the rich but to invite both rich and poor around a table at which they eat their fill at home with one another, with God, and within God's good creation.

The inverse of the rich man's estrangement from Lazarus is found in the parable Jesus has just told about a dishonest manager in 16:1-9. These two parables are intimately connected; the block of teaching from which the parable of Lazarus and the rich man comes is prompted by the Pharisees (glossed as lovers of money) mocking Jesus about the dishonest manager and the conclusions he draws (v. 14). The dishonest manager reveals an alternative use of wealth that leads not to alienation but to welcome.

The main character in this parable is a "manager," either a slave or a freedman charged with the taking care of a rich man's wealth. This manager is suspected of "squandering" his master's wealth (the Greek word is the same as in the parable of the prodigal in Luke 15:13, further tying together these three parables). As a result, the master tells the manager to give an accounting of his work and he'll be fired. The manager, however, has a plan. As he wraps up his final accounting, he cuts deals with the master's various debtors, slashing their debts, "so that," he reasons, "when I am dismissed as manager, people may welcome me into their homes" (16:4).

The manager, as his Greek title, *oikonomos*, suggests, demonstrates tremendous insight into what we might call "the laws of home." He recognizes that wealth is valuable, but only instrumentally. What lasts is membership in homes, the embrace of hospitality. His stroke of genius is to leverage ephemeral wealth for a much more durable mode of mutual belonging. Jesus commends the steward's insight, summarizing: "And I tell you, make friends for yourselves by means of dishonest wealth so that when it is gone, they may welcome you into the eternal homes" (16:9). The kingdom alchemy of the dishonest manager can be summarized as leveraging *houses* and the wealth they represent for entry into *homes*.

———

This is what the rich man has failed to do in his relationship with Lazarus. Had he invited Lazarus to join him at his table—even more, had he welcomed this unhoused man into his house—Lazarus would have been waiting for him in the world to come. Instead, the estrangement between Lazarus and the rich man endures eternally.

All this seems to come as a distressing surprise to the rich man. It is not a surprise to Abraham, and, when the rich man asks Abraham to send Lazarus to warn his brothers, Abraham insists that there is nothing new to tell the brothers: "They have Moses and the prophets; they should

listen to them" (16:29). The Jubilee ethic Jesus declared fulfilled in Luke 4 has long been available to them: "to share
your bread with the hungry, and bring the homeless poor
into your house" (Isa 58:7). The rich man insists that the
prophets will not suffice but that "if someone goes to them
from the dead, they will repent" (Luke 16:30). As seemed to
be the case of Simon the Pharisee, the rich man finds himself outside of the broad invitation to the table because he
cannot recognize his sin. Inasmuch as he has failed to share
his bread and welcome him into his house, the rich man has
sinned against Lazarus. But he cannot recognize it. And, he
fears, his brothers won't be able to, either. Abraham has the
final word: "If they do not listen to Moses and the prophets,
neither will they be convinced even if someone rises from
the dead" (v. 31).

Of course, as Luke tells it, we ourselves have one raised
from the dead: Jesus. And the rich are not persuaded—if by
"rich" we mean those who are attached to wealth as to a god.
Evidence and reason alone do not suffice to change idola-
trous attachment. Regarding Moses and the prophets, Abraham's insistence is typical for Luke: the Hebrew scriptures
are sufficient as revelations of the way of Jesus, as Jesus insists
in his own voice between these two parables in chapter 16
(vv. 16-17). Even when the one raised from the dead appears,
he explains himself by way of interpreting "Moses and all the
prophets" (24:27). The rich man has no excuse; the law and the
prophets are sufficient as revelations of the way of the Christ.

――――

The longed-for feast of the kingdom, which we see only in
(often-broken) pieces in these various parables, begins with

an eschatological repayment of earthly hospitality. In this life, those who find themselves wealthy invite the poor to their tables and welcome the unhoused into their houses. In the world to come, the poor (who are no longer poor, having benefited from the full realization of Jubilee) return the favor, inviting those who hosted them to *their* tables, welcoming them into eternal homes. Initiated through this eschatological return of hospitality, the formerly rich and formerly poor are then at home with one another at the great banquet of the kingdom.

With a long view to the feast of the kingdom of God, the invitation for the reader is to begin to enter into genuine relationships of mutual belonging with our eschatological tablemates. In this world in which wealth and honor are both distributed ever less equally, this move toward symmetric mutuality lays asymmetric demands on rich and poor. The first move in this eschatological exchange awaits those with wealth to steward right now. The wise move is to invite those who cannot now invite you back so that, "on that day," those who could not repay you will welcome you into eternal homes. Luke leaves us to ask ourselves: Whom will we welcome now? Who will welcome us later?

DISCUSSION QUESTIONS

1. With whom do you share your meals? What do you hope to get out of the exchange?

2. Is there estrangement in your relationships with those who have less than you do? Is there sin of which you need to repent?

3. When you engage across the lines of class, do these encounters deepen the divisions or break them down? Do

those who have more and those who have less relate as patrons and clients or as housemates-to-be? What would it look like to relate as "kin"?

4. How can our meals become sites of reconciliation that aim at life everlasting at home with one another, rich and poor?

5. How can our homes become sites of reconciliation that aim at life everlasting with one another, rich and poor?

PRAYER

Lord, let this be our piety: to loose the bonds of injustice, to undo the thongs of the yoke, to let the oppressed go free, and to break every yoke. Let us share our bread with the hungry and bring the homeless poor into our houses. When we see the naked, let us cover them. Let us not hide ourselves from our own kin, that we may welcome and be welcomed by one another as members of Your household. Amen. (Adapted from Isa 58:6-7.)

5

Dining at Home

Luke 22:1-30

At this point, the rich purpose of meals in Luke's Gospel is becoming clear. A meal is a site of nourishing mutual encounter among (a) people—rich and poor, sinners all; (b) places—both the dwellings where meals happen and the fields and wilds whence food comes; and (c) God—as the Creator of the people, the dwellings, the fields, and the wilds and as reconciler of all to one another in drawing all together toward consummation as the home of God.

———

Throughout Luke, when it has come to the meals, Jesus' main concerns are precisely these three things: the people, the places, and the presence of God. Let's begin with the people. When he eats a meal, Jesus wants to know: Who are the people at the table? Have the poor been invited? (14:12-24) Have the rich been disabused of their obsessions with status and power such that they can be present for nourishing mutual encounter with those gathered at the table and with God? (14:7-11) Are rich and poor together entering into the exchange of hospitality that marks entrance into the kingdom of God? (16:1-31) Do those gathered at the table know themselves as sinners called to repentance? (5:29-32) Has forgiveness received given birth to the profound love that allows us to draw near to God and to one another in the enduring mutuality of being at home? (7:31-50)

The places in which meals occur are also significant for Jesus. Because meals are not self-standing sites of nourishing mutual encounter as might happen in a coffee shop or a restaurant but rather enactments of *home*, when Jesus invites to the table, Jesus wants folks to ask: In whose home do we belong? His ministry is in this respect a persistent mission that aims to expand the reach—the "territory"—of God's home among mortals. We see this mission in Jesus' encounter with a chief tax collector, Zacchaeus. Seeing Zacchaeus, Jesus says baldly: "I must stay at your house today" (19:5). In Luke, this word, "must" (Gk. *dei*), routinely marks necessities of the divine plan (cf. 2:49; 4:43; 9:22; 13:33; 17:25; 21:9; 22:37; 24:7, 26, 44). Staying in Zacchaeus' home is essential to Jesus' mission. Zacchaeus hurries down to welcome him. "All who saw it began to grumble and said, 'He has gone to be the guest of one who is a sinner'" (19:7). But Jesus persists in his mission: this home is one to which he has been sent in order to help craft it *as* a home, to align it with the eschatological home (19:10). Likewise, it is not merely food but a *home* that draws the prodigal from his wayward wandering (15:11-32) and *homes* that the dishonest manager values over wealth (16:1-9). Conversely, the "un-homed" nature of certain homes interrupts meals (7:31-50, 14:7-11, 15:11-32). Jesus' mission is to prepare the land, prepare it to become what it was created to be and for which it was set aside as Israel's inheritance: a home for God and God's people.

Finally, in every meal, Jesus is turning our attention to God's purposes in them. God's purposes are for our mutual encounter and at-homeness with one another. But that full at-homeness is possible only through God's presence in the midst of these encounters. And so, at critical moments of Luke's Gospel, we find Jesus blessing and giving thanks to God for bread. He does so first at the feeding of the 5,000 (9:12-17). And he does so in two additional crucial moments at the ends of Luke's Gospel. In the Last Supper, he gives thanks for the cup and for the bread. This posture of gratitude and blessing before these essential gifts of God are so quintessentially Jesus that, at Emmaus, seeing him bless and break bread opens his tablemates' eyes (24:30-31).

————

In the climactic meal of Luke's Gospel, the Last Supper, God is quite clearly the One who has provided both the people and the places invited into nourishing mutual encounter. It is clear in 6:12-16 that it is God who calls together the community of disciples. Jesus goes up on a mountain to pray without even the idea, so far as the reader knows, of appointing a particular group of twelve from among the crowds he has been gathering. He returns with divine sanction to call *these* twelve, rich and poor (Levi the tax collector and Simon, Andrew, and John the fishermen), sworn enemies reconciled (Levi the turncoat and Simon the Zealot). They are, as are all of Jesus' tablemates, sinners, every last one. From the start, the disciples have distinguished themselves *as* disciples in acknowledging their sin and their need of repentance. Levi's call to discipleship is summarized by Jesus as a call to repentance (5:32). Simon's first step in discipleship is to declare: "I am a sinful man!" (5:8b). As far as Simon has come in his discipleship, this final night, as Jesus predicts at the table, he will deny Jesus three times (22:34).

In 6:16, we are warned that Jesus' decision to draw near to sinners will have its consequences, as Judas is named from the start as one who would become a traitor. As the various people and pieces come together for the Last Supper, we are ominously reminded again of this fact (22:3-6). Judas has chosen to betray Jesus for an unspecified sum of money, proving the truth of Jesus' teaching in 16:13: "You cannot serve God and wealth." This was the teaching offered between the parable of the dishonest manager and the parable of Lazarus and the rich man—the parables of the stakes of home, forged or eternally lost through the ways we use wealth. The dishonest manager is commended for winning friends through the use of dishonest wealth such that he may be welcomed into new homes. Judas betrays a friend for the sake of dishonest wealth and risks losing Jesus' invitation to be at home with him. But, as the scene is set in

Luke 22, Judas is present, a sinner—a betrayer—whom Jesus the Jubilee herald has continued to invite to the table.

The place, too, Luke tells us, is provided by God. Jesus asks Peter and John to make preparations for the Passover meal. The dialogue is reminiscent of the prelude to the feeding of the 5,000, but, instead of lacking *food*, they lack a *place* for the meal. The Son of Man, after all, has nowhere to lay his head (9:58). As in Luke 9:14-16, Jesus gives them specific instructions to follow, and miraculous provision follows. Bread issuing from the mouth of the Lord in this case includes a guest room where the unleavened bread of the Passover can be eaten.

The context of the Passover itself reminds us of a larger sense in which God has provided the place for this meal. The Passover sacrifice is to be offered "at the place that the LORD will choose as a dwelling for his name" (Deut 16:2). Deuteronomy goes on to insist twice more (vv. 5-7) that the sacrifice is only to be made in the place the Lord will choose. Ever since Luke 9:51, "[w]hen the days drew near for him to be taken up" and so Jesus "set his face to go to Jerusalem," the inevitability of this place and what is to happen here has loomed over the Gospel. To the extent that we are to understand the death of Christ in Luke as a Passover sacrifice, Jerusalem is central to the story Luke is telling as the place where "the Passover lamb had to be sacrificed" (22:7).

But the Passover also speaks in a broader sense to God's miraculous provision of Canaan in the Exodus. The field in which Jesus and his disciples were plucking grain on the Sabbath is in a double sense a gift from God: God created it, and God set it aside for God's people. The Sea of Galilee from which Simon drew the miraculous catch of fish is just this as well. As the anointed-but-not-yet-enthroned king, Jesus has been traveling this God-created and God-given countryside, routing the enemies of the people: spiritual oppression, disease, and the like. He has been liberating the land from which comes the food on the table this night, preparing the land to become the home it was created and given to be.

————

The scene set, the meal begins. Jesus takes his place at the table, the apostles with him. As in chapter 14, the occasion of the meal prompts a concern about status. While Luke postpones the dispute until after the meal (22:24-27), the prior incident suggests that the dispute may have been occasioned by the crisis of status brought on by the need to occupy particular positions at the table. In chapter 14, Jesus offered wise counsel on how to navigate the status game played by those jockeying for social position in Roman Judea. Here, he lays out an entirely different status economy that is to operate among the disciples: "the greatest among you must become like the youngest, and the leader like one who serves" (22:26). Jesus points to his own status at the table as one who serves as the example they should follow.

Jesus' posture is a model of how we ought to serve one another around our tables, and, by extension, as we live toward the sorts of homes our tables can call forth. As sites of nourishing mutual encounter, meals are sites of mutual care. In a world in which striving for honor and status disrupts this mutuality of care, there is a need for someone to initiate, to offer care without guarantee of reciprocation. That is, in a world like ours, there is need to dare *sacrificial* service on behalf of those with whom God is inviting us to be at home. Jesus' servant posture at the table is a model of how to live into a world of mutuality while still awash in a world obsessed with status. Like Jesus, we are invited to commit to sacrificial service in the context of and in the service of the hope of abundant life with God. Sometimes, our imitative acts of service will inaugurate new modalities of mutual belonging and, in so doing, become partial and fleeting—but nevertheless precious—realizations of the eschatological home in the here and now. Often our acts of sacrificial service will seem to come up empty. In either case, they build in us the heart of service that is core to the way of life Jesus has commended to us.

The meal itself follows what we may suppose was the typical order for a first-century Palestinian Passover. For those inclined to read this meal simply as proto-Eucharist, especially striking is the presence of *two* cups (22:17-18, 20). The language of the cups—"a cup" in v. 17, "the cup after supper" in v. 20—assumes the structure of the Passover, with multiple cups and multiple moments of instruction about the significance of the meal. As throughout Luke, Jesus is again taking up language and symbolic structures of the Hebrew Bible and transforming them in order to offer insight into his identity and mission as Messiah.

With the first cup, Jesus marks the departure from the Passover script. He abstains, offering the cup instead *only* to his tablemates. In place of drinking, he articulates his commitment not to "drink of the fruit of the vine until the kingdom of God comes" (22:18). That eschatological feast that has served as a template for and topic of conversation at the Gospel's meals now draws near enough that Jesus declares a personal fast until it comes.

The bread, Jesus says, is his body, given for his disciples (22:19). Jesus has thus far been the one invited and inviting to the table. He has been the one preparing the land and the people for nourishing mutual encounter. At this final meal, Jesus is revealed also as the bread to be eaten. His body is the unleavened bread that leads to liberation. But it is also more than this. As we noted already, the manner in which Jesus deals with the bread, taking it, giving thanks, breaking it, and giving it, recalls to mind both the feeding of the 5,000 and the provision of manna in the desert invoked by that story. With this accumulating set of images in mind, in declaring that the bread is his body, Jesus declares himself to be the manna from heaven. Jesus is himself that bread that comes from his mouth (Deut 8:3), a miracle that is happening as he speaks these words we now know as the words of institution.

In revealing Jesus as the bread on the table, Luke does not negate, but rather builds upon, all he has said thus far. This body that is offered to us as bread is the body that fed 5,000 and invited sinners to the table. This is the body that declared the Jubilee and invited rich and poor together at the table. This is the body that gave itself for the life of the world on the cross and the body that rose in glory. This is the body of Jesus' story, but it is still *body* and therefore eating of it is an affirmation of creation as such and of that part of God's creation that was Jesus' life in the body. This body—not only the story that it invokes—is present to us in the Eucharistic Bread. It is the Bread of Christ's living presence with us. This Bread of ours is more important than any ordinary bread, but it includes material bread for all. This is why those who follow Jesus say that when we eat of this Bread, we, too, become little Christs—Christians—to the world, inviting the world to be at home with God, who is remaking the world through this Christ at work within us.

In the Last Supper and the crucifixion it figures, this Bread is broken and *given for us* (22:19). This manna comes at a cost. Jesus' practice of service is sacrificial. As a result, the Last Supper and the Lord's Supper that it inaugurates are feasts of celebration and mourning intermingled. It is a Passover meal, a celebration of remembrance and enactment of liberation. But the bread we eat is the Bread of Jesus' suffering body; in this sense it is bitter bread. And so, if and when we eat the Eucharistic meal, we celebrate the liberation and also mourn its cost.

With the second cup, Jesus interprets the cup as he has the bread: "This cup that is poured out for you is the new covenant in my blood" (22:20). The language of "new covenant" calls to mind Jeremiah 31:31-34. There, the new covenant is marked by the integration of intimate knowledge of God and God's law into the self (v. 32) and the forgiveness of sins (v. 34). Jeremiah 31, however, does not contain any reference to blood. The inclusion of blood harkens to Exodus 24:8, in which Moses ratifies the Sinaitic covenant, dashing blood from the offerings on the people, saying, "See the blood of the covenant that the LORD has made with you in accordance with all these words." However new this covenant is (and Jer 31:32 distinguishes the new covenant from the one made at Sinai), it is still of the same genus as the original: it is a covenant between God and God's people, initiated by God, dependent only on God's faithfulness, and ratified through the shedding of blood (Meyers, 205–8). As Richard Hays notes, the context of a meal is also shared with this intertext from Exodus 24, where vv. 9-11 recount Moses, Aaron, and the elders of Israel sharing a meal in the presence of the God of Israel. Exodus twice says these leaders *saw* the God of Israel (vv. 10, 11) and yet were not harmed. At the Lord's Supper, too, the disciples eat and drink in the presence of God (Hays, 134). Even more, they eat and drink *of* God broken, given, and poured out for them.

By the end of the meal, then, we have a fuller sense of what this posture of service which is commended to us might entail. At the table, the significance of Jesus' invitation in Luke 9:23 comes into focus: "If any want to become my followers, let them deny themselves and take up their cross daily and follow me." To be clear: Jesus' sacrificial service is not merely for our remembrance but for our imitation. Perhaps many Christians have allowed this shocking phrase, "let them take up their cross daily," to become too familiar to us. This is a call to radical service, to risk even death for the sake of the other—even more, for the sake of abundant life at home with the other and with God. This is the way of life to which we commit ourselves at the

Eucharistic table—and at any table we allow to become for us the Lord's table.

————

After these familiar moments focused on the bread and cup, after another ominous mention of the unnamed traitor in their midst (22:21-23), and after the dispute about status (22:24-27), Jesus invites his disciples to eat and drink at his table in the consummated kingdom of God (22:28-30). As at many meals prior, so, too, at this climactic meal: the meal finds its ultimate significance in its relationship to the feast of the kingdom. From the many meals and feasts of the Gospel of Luke, Jesus commits to a fast until the eschatological feast. With this full arc in view, this moment invites us to consider what we have learned about this generative tension between feasting and fasting running throughout the meals of Luke's Gospel.

To this point in Luke's Gospel, many of Jesus' meals, his "feasting," have been in the mode of the "true fast" of Isaiah 58. Taken together, the meals have been sites where Jesus has loosed the bonds of injustice, shared bread with the hungry, and welcomed the homeless poor into houses. And this climactic meal continues just this, inasmuch as Jesus' disciples themselves are rich and poor, sinners all, called to the good news of Jubilee: forgiveness of sins, of debts, and an invitation to be at home at the feast of the kingdom of God. Throughout Luke, Isaiah's true *fast* is enacted in the *feasting* of Jesus and his followers.

In this scene, however, we can discern the enduring distinction between these two modes, feasting and fasting.

The Last Supper is a feast inasmuch as it is a rehearsal for and partial realization of the eschatological banquet yet to come. But it is also a fast inasmuch as it is decidedly *not yet* that eschatological feast. Jesus calls out this sense in which this feast is a fast when he commits to abstaining from the Passover meal until it is fulfilled in the kingdom (22:16). Now begins his time of fasting; now begins the time of fasting he foretold in 5:35, when the bridegroom is taken away. The nature of the bridegroom's departure—with broken body and blood poured out—presents the Last Supper also as a fast in two other senses: a fast of mourning and of sacrifice. Inasmuch as they understand the bread as Jesus' body broken and given for them, the disciples mourn as they partake. Inasmuch as they understand the connection between Jesus' fast from the Passover until its fulfillment in the kingdom and his offering of himself *for them*, the fast Jesus begins and into which the disciples enter (5:35) is one that commits them to living in imitation of his self-giving love.

In Eucharist, we, too, are invited both to feast and to fast. Those who partake feast, as Paul suggests (1 Cor 5:8), in realizing here and now the way of *love* that is the way of the coming kingdom. We eat the bread of Christ's story, and, as the bread becomes part of our material bodies, we seek for Christ's story to become the fundamental structure of our own. We "discern the body" (1 Cor 11:29) gathered at the table, rich and poor, sinners all, and we recognize in this body the very Body of Christ in the world. But we also fast, as we anticipate the fullness of the kingdom not yet present among us. We come to the Lord's Supper longing for the kingdom that we, with our perishable flesh and blood, cannot yet inherit (1 Cor 15:50). We come longing for that moment in which we are all changed and put on immortality (1 Cor 15:51-53). We mourn as we eat the body broken and drink of the blood poured out. We commit ourselves to the way of Christ in self-giving love for the sake of the other with whom God has called us to be at home.

But the Eucharist is not the only site of this dynamic of feasting and fasting. In our whole lives we are to feast and to fast. Our tables are—always at least potentially—sites of partial realization of the eschatological banquet. They are places where the new home God is calling forth comes to be—in part, incompletely, and only for a time. Should we answer Jesus' call, our tables can become places where rich and poor belong to one another, where, sinners all, we repent and gather to be healed by Jesus, who came to set us free, and we celebrate the joy of repentance and the joy of Jubilee freedom.

Even as we feast in this way—normed by and in hopeful anticipation of the eschatological home to come—our feasting is always marked by incompleteness, because, in this world, the home such feasts enact is in some ways *foreign* to the contexts in which it is coming to be. All homes are embedded within larger contexts—economic, political, cultural, ecological. In the world to come, these contexts will be transformed: individuals and nations will be reconciled to one another; those who have no money will come and buy (Isa 55:1); the wolf and the lamb will live together in peace (Isa 11:6-9). For now, these contexts are not yet transformed—and will not be until the end of all things. As a result, these profound moments and spaces of at-homeness are always limited by the fact that their larger contexts are "unfitting." In this light, even our feasts are fasts. As we encounter the joy of being for a moment and in a corner at home with one another, with the world, and with God, we are brought up short by this home's lack of fit with the world around us, and, for just that reason, we long for that world in which this moment and this corner extend everywhere and into life everlasting.

For this reason, Christians also fast. For certain times, we abstain from food altogether. We do so not because food is bad and hunger is good. We do so not because food is good but God is better. We do so because, to paraphrase theologian Norman Wirzba, food is God's love made delectable, and we long to live in that love at home with one another and with God in a world of perfect love (7, 180). When we fast, we join with Jesus in expressing our longing, our hunger for that meal, in that home, at that time, and in that world remade.

And we fast because food is God's love made delectable for the *other*. We refrain from eating so that others can eat. We refrain from eating to enter into solidarity with those who have nothing to eat. We fast in order to cultivate in ourselves a posture that holds space for the other. We fast as a discipline that allows God to form within us the way of the cross—the way of the everlasting home in the midst of a world un-homed and in the process of being re-homed. We fast precisely in order to become the sort of people who welcome others to tables and into homes where the home of God is coming to be in our midst.

DISCUSSION QUESTIONS

1. How would thinking about your meals as nourishing mutual encounters between people, places, and the presence of God change: the way you eat? what you eat? where you eat? with whom you eat?

2. What contexts around you are particularly "unfitting" to the home that God is bringing about in your midst? What economic, political, cultural, and ecological dynamics do you long to see transformed? Consider doing a fast from food (only if and as it is safe and healthy for you to do so) as a way of investing your body in this longing for transformation and for the world to become God's home.

PRAYER

Jesus, we long to eat at Your table in Your kingdom. Prepare us now for the fellowship that awaits us there. Deposit in us Your way of love and of service to our neighbors. Prepare us now for the world remade. Deposit in us Your way of love and service to the fields and wilds of the world You created. Prepare us now for the home into which we are invited. Grow in us a longing for the world at home in having become Your home. May we hunger and thirst for the feast that awaits us in the home You have prepared. Amen.

6

Made Known
in the Breaking
of the Bread

Luke 24:1-43, 10:38-42

After the Last Supper, what has been looming over the Gospel unfolds apace. Jesus is captured, tried, and crucified. The one who abstained from the cup at the Passover, vowing not to drink of the fruit of the vine again until the kingdom of God comes, has a new cup to drink, one the Father will not remove (22:42). The kiss Jesus was denied by Simon the Pharisee, received liberally from the woman who knew herself forgiven, is now delivered ironically by Judas the traitor (22:47-48). Jesus' prediction at the table of Peter's denial comes to pass (22:54-62).

For Luke, the Gospel of symposia, feasts, snacks on the go, and meals among friends, the cross is a *fast*. Sour wine is offered (23:36), but mockingly. The offer of the peasant's drink is meant to pair ironically with the sign declaring him "King of the Jews." The scene calls to mind David's lament in Psalm 69:21: "for my thirst they gave me vinegar to drink." On the cross, Jesus persists in the fast he began at the Seder, not to partake again until the kingdom of God comes. And Luke is at great pains to remind us that, inasmuch as Jesus' death is unjust, the justice of the kingdom of God has hardly arrived. Pilate three times says he finds no fault in him (23:4, 14, 22). One of the criminals crucified with him admits his own guilt but testifies to Jesus' innocence (23:41). And yet he is crucified. The centurion, who in Mark and Matthew declares him the Son of God, in Luke concludes "this man was innocent" (23:47). It seems that injustice has the final word. The kingdom lies in tatters and appears not to have come at all. Jesus fasts.

Nevertheless, Jesus continues his Jubilee ministry on the cross. If we take 23:34a to be authentic, Jesus forgives even those crucifying him, demonstrating his teaching from 6:28b, "pray for those who abuse you." And he promises the confessing criminal a home with him in paradise (23:43). But Jesus does not set himself free, though goaded by the jeering onlookers to do so (23:37, 39). As a righteous elder of the people lays him in a tomb (23:53) and the women who had been following him prepare the body for burial (23:55-56), Jesus is captive to the tomb—a captive yet awaiting release.

———

After an intervening Sabbath, Mary Magdalene, Joanna, and Mary the mother of James return to the tomb and find it empty (24:1-3). The angels urge them to remember Jesus' teaching about how it had to be for the Son of Man (24:4-7). The women remember and share the good news with the male disciples (24:8-10). The male disciples are unimpressed (24:11). Peter, at least, is willing to give it a look (24:12), but the work of interpreting the empty tomb is very much still in process when Luke cuts away to a different scene, one only Luke records (24:13-35).

Two unnamed disciples are walking from Jerusalem to Emmaus, a village not far away. They're talking about the arrest, trial, crucifixion, and reports of the empty tomb. As they're talking, Jesus begins walking along with them, but they are kept from recognizing him. It is a classic Gospel problem: people see Jesus but do not recognize him. From the early errant musings of the crowds reported to Herod and through the disciples to Jesus to the misconstruals of Jesus' identity at the trials, again and again, people see but do not perceive (8:10). Now these misrecognitions, which happen in the minds of various characters in the story, are played out literally in narrative form: Jesus is present but hidden from sight.

Jesus innocently asks what they're talking about. They stand still. Surely, they remark, he's the only person in Jerusalem not caught up in the drama of the past few days. They catch him up. After narrating to the point of the crucifixion, they lament, "But we had hoped that he was the one to redeem Israel" (24:21). They *had* hoped. Few things are as heart-wrenching as the consignment of hope to the past tense. The weight of this hope has been building from the very beginning of the Gospel. Zechariah's hymn speaks of God's redeeming Israel (1:68). Anna the prophetess' wait for the redemption of Jerusalem is fulfilled in encountering the child Jesus in the temple (2:38). Beyond these specific invocations of the language of redemption, the entire infancy narrative is driven not by the personal stories of Mary and Elizabeth and Zechariah but by the fervent hope for the *people* of God. John the Baptist "will turn many of the people of Israel to the Lord their God" (1:16). Jesus "will reign over the house of Jacob forever" (1:33). The good news of the birth is announced as "good news of great joy for all the people"—that is, first and foremost, the whole people of Israel (2:10). Simeon speaks to this mission to the people and then to the nations, naming Jesus as "a light for revelation to the Gentiles and for glory to your people Israel" (2:32). Even the diction itself in the infancy narrative speaks to the summation of the hopes of Israel in God's activity in this young boy. The first two chapters are written in the style of the Greek translation of the Hebrew Bible. To capture the effect in English, we should probably read Luke 1–2 in the King James Version and then switch to a modern translation somewhere before we arrive in Luke 4. The point is to steep the reader in the sense that what is unfolding is sacred history, a continuation of the account of God's interaction with God's people, Israel. The disciples' hope for the redemption of Israel is well-founded indeed.

After they finish narrating the story through to the empty tomb, Jesus urges them to return to the scriptures: "'Was it not necessary that the Messiah should suffer these things and then enter into his glory?' Then beginning with Moses and all the prophets, he interpreted to them the things about himself in all the scriptures" (24:26-27). Perhaps he began with Isaiah 58 and 61, his Jubilee mission. Or perhaps he began with the lesson of the manna in the wilderness. Doubtless, he reminded them of the suffering servant of Isaiah 53, whom he had invoked as they left the table that last night (Luke 22:37). Surely he retold the story of David and his mission as one anointed-but-not-yet-enthroned. Even more, given what Luke has told us, he pointed them to the Psalms. As Joshua Jipp highlights, Luke uses multiple Davidic psalms—not just the citations of Psalm 22 (Luke 23:34b) and Psalm 31 (Luke 23:46), but also the subtler gestures toward Psalm 38 (compare Ps 38:11 and Luke 23:49a) and Psalm 89 (compare Ps 89:3, 19-20 and Luke 23:35b)—to depict Jesus as the suffering Davidic king. Recalling what we learned in the grainfields, we can specify further: Jesus is the Davidic figure suffering unjustly because his kingship is disputed in the yawning gap between his anointing and his enthronement. The anointed one suffers before entering into glory because his presence *as* the anointed of God amidst the regnant way of injustice provokes violent opposition. If he is to embrace those who violently oppose him, the Messiah will have first to suffer unjustly at their hands. This is consistent throughout Luke-Acts: Jesus dies for us *at our hands* (Acts 2:36, 4:10).

Suffice it to say: Jesus *is* the one come to redeem Israel—he is, in fact, the *Lord* come to redeem Israel. The story these two followers have narrated is not a disappointment of that expectation but rather its fulfillment. Jesus is the Messiah, the anointed one in the lineage of David. His Jubilee mission has met its inevitably violent opposition. The cross is not disconfirming evidence but rather confirmation of that identity. The resurrection speaks to God's vindication of the One unjustly killed. Not even violent opposition can overcome God's pursuit of humanity through the Jubilee king.

Powerful as this exposition of scripture must have been—later the companions note that their hearts were "burning within" as he opened the scriptures to them (Luke 24:32)—it is not the moment when the two disciples recognize Jesus. That comes later, after they ask him to stay with them. The scene should be familiar to us: They invite Jesus into their home for a meal. At the table, roles reverse, and Jesus becomes host: "he took bread, blessed and broke it, and gave it to them" (24:30). It is at this moment that "their eyes were opened, and they recognized him" (24:31). It is in this intimate space (a simple meal in a village home) and in this simple act (the blessing and breaking of bread) that Jesus is revealed. In assuming the role of host, Jesus transforms their home into God's home, and they recognize him. Presumably they recognize that feeling of being at home as it was enacted in that meal, that life-giving mutual encounter between the land whose liberation they had just celebrated in Passover, the house to which they had journeyed, the God to whom thanks is due, and the people, particularly *this* man, Jesus, who had welcomed them to the table so many times before.

We don't know at which meals these companions might have been with Jesus. They haven't been named elsewhere in the Gospel. But as readers, all the Gospel's meals come rushing back: The rowdy feast with Levi and his "sinner" friends. The meal at Zacchaeus' place, where Jesus *had* to be hosted. The meal at Simon the Pharisee's house with the woman who truly *recognized* Jesus. Most of all, the feeding of the 5,000 where Jesus *blessed and broke* the loaves and the fish, and the Passover Seder just days before where Jesus *gave thanks and broke* the bread, offering his body for us.

When these companions return to Jerusalem to report to the apostles, one feature serves to summarize the whole: Jesus "had been made known to them in the breaking of the bread" (24:35). As he has been to us.

———

Even as the apostles are still talking about the Emmaus revelation, it is repeated. Jesus appears in their midst. Again, he is misrecognized; this time, he is taken to be a ghost. Jesus shows his wounds. The disciples are unconvinced. Again, food is the key. Jesus asks if they have anything to eat. He eats a piece of broiled fish in their presence. This act, presumably, demonstrates that Jesus is not a ghost. As throughout Luke, eating is the quintessential action of a human being. A ghost who can eat is no ghost; this is a human being in flesh and bones.

Thus, we have a third pairing of bread and fish—the basic meal of Jesus' Galilean home. At the beginning of the Gospel, we saw the bread in the temptation and the miraculous catch of fish in the calling of Simon. At the feeding of the 5,000, we have bread and fish at once. And finally we have bread at Emmaus and fish in Jerusalem in these two post-resurrection appearances. Even while eating, Jesus is the Lord from whose mouth comes bread and fish and every good gift, come to be with us, made known to us in the basic material gifts of God's creation: God's love made delectable in food that sustains our bodies and draws us to the table at which we are at home with one another and with God.

After eating in their presence, Jesus then repeats the Emmaus road Bible lesson, interpreting everything written about himself "in the law of Moses, the prophets, and the psalms" (24:44). The inclusion of the Psalms in this list is notable and lends credence to our hunch above that the Psalms are central to the scriptures that attest to the need for the Messiah to suffer, be crucified, and be raised again. The Hebrew scriptures are sufficient for the proclamation of Jesus the Messiah. But they require Jesus to interpret them; this time Luke vividly describes Jesus "open[ing] their minds to understand the scriptures" (24:45).

Each time, these post-resurrection appearances pair the two: the food and the word. On the road to Emmaus, the word comes first: the necessity of the Messiah to suffer, die, and be raised. Then comes the food, by which that suffering and glorified Messiah is revealed to be this man, Jesus, the living bodily presence in their home. In Jerusalem, first comes the food: the resurrected body in their midst is revealed to be Jesus, whom Peter had confessed as Messiah.

Then comes the word, by which this word, "Messiah," is prevented from becoming an empty signifier. This anointed herald of the abundant Jubilee life with God has offered his body and blood *for them*. He has died and been raised to new life. His Jubilee mission continues: "repentance and forgiveness of sins is to be proclaimed in his name to all nations, beginning from Jerusalem" (24:47), and, as Acts will demonstrate, extending to the ends of the earth, until the whole earth is at home in having become the home of God. Then all will feast in the kingdom of God.

———

To the pious mind, there is something almost galling about the way Luke pairs food and the word in these passages. Surely, scripture is primary. It can seem that piety demands that we elevate the spiritual over the physical. But Luke is insistent that recognizing the primacy of the word of God does not demand we demean the good gifts that flow from the mouth of the Lord. Choosing between bread and the Lord by whose word bread comes is always a false choice.

There is one very famous meal in Luke we haven't yet discussed that was understood for centuries as demanding that we make exactly this choice. As so many others, Mary and Martha welcome Jesus into their home (Luke 10:38-42). Like the Zacchaeus encounter, the meal that must surely have been at the center of this hospitality is not explicitly mentioned. Nevertheless, the material reality of hospitality pervades the short episode. As Luke tells it, Martha is "distracted by her many tasks." Mary sits at the feet of Jesus. When Martha asks Jesus to intervene, he answers: "Martha,

Martha, you are worried and distracted by many things; there is need of only one thing. Mary has chosen the better part, which will not be taken away from her" (10:41-42).

From Origen to Augustine and forward, Martha and Mary were taken to represent a contrast between two ways of life: the active and the contemplative, the life of the flesh and the life of the Spirit, the labors of this life and the Sabbath rest of the life to come (Schüssler-Fiorenza, 58–62). On this reading, we have to choose: hospitality or discipleship, the world or the Lord, the bread or the word. Only one thing is necessary.

But this reading essentially grants the false choice with which the devil began his temptation of Christ: food or the Lord. It hears in Jesus' response to Martha what he refuses to say to the devil: *the human does not live by bread.* Jesus does not deny the necessity, or even the goodness, of bread in the temptation. And he does not deny the value of hospitality at the table in his encounter with Martha. To the contrary, as we noted in our discussion of the Last Supper, Jesus elevates table service as an icon of his ministry.

Only one thing is necessary. It is true. But this one thing is not God as opposed to the worldly home. The one thing is the word of Jesus through which the world came to be and through which the world comes to be more than *mere* world. The presence of God in Jesus Christ is therefore precisely the "better part," but not as victor over the worldly home as if it were God's competition—rather, as the one with whom we find ourselves truly at home, in whose presence the world truly becomes home by being more than *merely* the world. Granted, we do not live by our worldly homes alone any more than we do by bread alone. But, just as we are not to live without bread, we are not to live without the world. The one thing necessary is to know Jesus precisely as the one in whom every good thing is united. As God-man, Jesus is the one through whom all created goods are revealed not to be competitors to God. Rather, all created goods are most fully themselves as created goods in relationship to God and to the world whose consummation as the home of God Jesus inaugurates. This is what Mary most gets right. She recognizes in the material realities of meal preparation and hospitality sacraments of the kingdom—but only if they find they are oriented around One who has come proclaiming and demonstrating the kingdom coming.

To be sure, Jesus' affirmation of "the one thing" is a statement against any idealization of a home as a mere "thing," a space from which God is absent. Absent recognition of God's abiding and unifying presence, home can become just what it seems to be for Martha: dizzying concern for "so many things." Our lives may be just this; if so, it is a sign we have lost sight of the one thing.

The affirmation of the one thing is a statement against any vision of home in which God comes to be of interest only after the matters of household management (*oikonomia* in the Greek, from which we derive "economics") have been attended to. To miss God is to miss the home as well, just as to neglect God is to settle for mere bread and forgo the bread for which we truly hunger—bread that is more than bread.

Neither will this vision of home allow God to become an instrument of economy. We cannot appeal to Jesus as

Martha does on behalf of the home as opposed to God. This story, which directly precedes the Lord's Prayer, will not permit us to pray: "Lord, make us rich." Many would turn faith into just this sort of tool. To do so would be to drain even what wealth we have of its value.

No, in affirming the "one thing," Jesus affirms the unity expressed in his signature turn of phrase, "the kingdom of God." The kingdom of God is not kingdom alone; it is not the world apart from God. Nor is the kingdom of God God alone; it is not God apart from the world. The kingdom of God is these two together: God and the world at home with one another. Or better yet: the world at home in having become the home of God (Volf and Croasmun, 68–69).

When we long for home—and how we do long for true home!—we are also and first of all longing for God. That is not to say our longing for home is an illusion or an error. Our true longing is not for God *instead* of for home. When we long for home, we long for God in that we long for a home where God is not an add-on but rather constitutive of home and definitive of all the other relations that *really are* essential there. We long for a home where God is constitutive of our relationships with one another. Where we recognize that God is always already at work in the midst of our sin, our repentance, our forgiving one another, and our reconciliation—our hosting one another across dividing lines of class, ability, and ethnicity. We long for a home where God is constitutive of our relationships with the geographies around us. Where we name God as creator and consummator of the places we live, the land from which we draw our sustenance, the wilds that draw us to wonder. We long for a home where God is constitutive of our mutual belonging within our social and ecological worlds.

This is what is at stake in the meals of Luke's Gospel. Each meal is a sacrament of this union of God and the world. Each meal points to God's drawing the world to final consummation as the home of God, to which scripture testifies. The quintessential picture of this at-homeness is the *feast* of the kingdom; it is home *enacted*. Each meal we eat together—rich and poor, sinners all, at home with one another in the world God created and is drawing to consummation—can become a sacrament of that home coming to be in our midst.

Therefore, let us keep the feast.

DISCUSSION QUESTIONS

1. How has Jesus been made known to you as you've encountered him in the meals of Luke's Gospel?

2. When are you tempted to (a) see God as absent from your ideal picture of home, (b) imagine God as an "add-on" to your ideal vision of home, or (c) attempt to make God a tool you can use in service of your own goals?

3. What would it look like intentionally to plan a meal at which Jesus might be made known in the breaking of bread? If you've been reading this book together with a group, consider hosting a meal that gathers rich and poor, sinners all, to a meal that quite deliberately enacts that home to which God is inviting us. Consider what you will eat and the fields and wilds from which it comes. Consider the people around the table, how they can feel welcomed. Consider how you might bless and/or give

thanks for the meal; consider how the entire meal might be an experience of blessing and thanksgiving.

PRAYER

Lord, be for us the One in whom everything else finds its meaning. Be at the center of our meals. Be at the center of our homes. Fill our hearts with longing for the feast and for the home you have prepared for us. Make us attentive to that home and that feast as they come to be in our midst. Let us receive your kingdom with joy.

Acknowledgments

This short book has been a long time coming. In the fall of 2015, we read Luke alongside our "Christ and the Good Life" class at Yale Divinity School; it was with these sharp and curious students that we first started thinking about the prominence of the theme of food in Luke's Gospel. A weekly Bible study in 2016 and 2017 at the Elm City Vineyard Church in New Haven was for Matt another early source of insight and opportunity to sit patiently with Luke's text. A November 2017 Yale Center for Faith & Culture consultation on "Feasting and Fasting" convinced us of the fecundity of food as a site for reflection on life with God and with one another. That consultation was generously supported by the McDonald Agape Foundation and expertly hosted by Denise and Stephen Adams at their ADAMVS vineyard.

Ultimately, the book you hold in your hands was born from the weekly Bible study of the Yale Center for Faith & Culture, where, over a period of two years from 2019 to 2021, our colleagues, Ryan McAnnally-Linz, Drew Collins, and Angela Gorrell, lent their many profound insights and questions to the development not only of the text but of the concept as well. The project incubated for so long that, by the time the book itself was being drafted, Angela had moved to Baylor and it fell to Ryan and Drew to give their generous notes on the manuscript. Nathan Jowers provided transcription and editorial support.

We give thanks to God for all these friends and colleagues for their many contributions to the feast Luke has become for us over these years.

One final note: Along with several colleagues, we are working on an expansive series of books, each of which considers one or another aspect of human life in light of the life and work of Jesus Christ. We call each book a "Contribution to a Theology of Life." Together, they aim to present a vision of the flourishing of human beings and the whole creation in the presence of God and to sketch the kinds of life that might be lived in response to that vision. We have taken the "home of God" as a guiding biblical motif for that vision and thus "homemaking" as a central image for the journey. We did not exactly plan it this way, but, in the writing of this book, we realized that there is in Luke's Gospel a whole theology of food, eating, and their relation to homemaking and the home of God. So as it turned out, this book belongs with that larger project.

Works Cited

Assmann, Jan. *The Invention of Religion: Faith and Covenant in the Book of Exodus*. Princeton: Princeton University Press, 2020.

Bovon, François. *Luke 1: A Commentary on the Gospel of Luke 1:1–9:50*. Edited by Helmut Koester. Translated by Christine M. Thomas. Minneapolis: Fortress, 2002.

Green, Joel B. *The Gospel of Luke*. Grand Rapids: Eerdmans, 1997.

Hays, Richard B. *Echoes of Scripture in the Gospels*. Waco, Tex.: Baylor University Press, 2016.

Jipp, Joshua W. "Luke's Scriptural Suffering Messiah: A Search for Precedent, a Search for Identity." *Catholic Biblical Quarterly* 72, no. 2 (2010): 255–74.

Karris, Robert J. *Eating Your Way through Luke's Gospel*. Collegeville, Minn.: Liturgical Press, 2006.

Meyers, Carol. *Exodus*. New York: Cambridge University Press, 2005.

Schüssler-Fiorenza, Elizabeth. *But She Said: Feminist Practices of Biblical Interpretation*. Boston: Beacon, 1992.

Tonstad, Linn. *God and Difference: The Trinity, Sexuality, and the Transformation of Finitude*. New York: Routledge, 2015.

Volf, Miroslav, and Matthew Croasmun. *For the Life of the World: Theology That Makes a Difference*. Grand Rapids: Brazos, 2019.

Wirzba, Norman. *Food and Faith: A Theology of Eating*. New York: Cambridge University Press, 2018.